Eternal Love

Doreen S. Barber

ARCHWAY
PUBLISHING

Archway Publishing books may be ordered through booksellers or by contacting:

Archway Publishing
1663 Liberty Drive
Bloomington, IN 47403
www.archwaypublishing.com
1 (888) 242-5904

ISBN: 978-1-4808-2982-4 (sc)
ISBN: 978-1-4808-2983-1 (e)

Library of Congress Control Number: 2016905198

Print information available on the last page.

Archway Publishing rev. date: 08/04/2016

Contents

Foreword

There are nine Hebrew words for love. Their meanings cover everything from mental recognition to physical intimacy. The Greeks have fewer words for love but they use them to make necessary distinctions between the spiritual, interpersonal, philanthropic and erotic. English has just one word to cover such an expansive subject. Consequently, people think nothing of using it to convey devotion to the Lord, affection for a household pet, a preference for a particular flavor, or sexual perversion. One word fits all, but such convenience comes at a high price: it often diminishes the noble while elevating the base.

Yet if God is the author of love, as well as its perfection, we ought to endeavor to understand love better.

As Paul wrote, "And though I have the gift of prophecy, and understand all mysteries, and all knowledge; and though I have all faith, so that I could remove mountains, and have not love, I am nothing" (1 Corinthians 13: 2).

Like an understudy of Paul, Doreen Barber presents a stellar piece of scholarship. It is high time a book like this entered the Christian market. It is both professionally sound and Biblically based. I regret not having it when I was in private practice as a Counseling Therapist.

Wilfred Kent DMin, PhD Chancellor
International College of Behavior Counseling

Acknowledgments

To Jesus, who calls me 'His Friend' – all glory and honor belongs to Him as He spoke, guided and lead me through this endeavor. The process was a joy and delight.

My husband, Gary, who had to patiently wait many hours alone as I completed this book, though he always knew right where to find me. His patience, unconditional love and support were a divine gift of biblical proportions.

To Karen who prayed and supported my endeavor. Her devotion and revelation added an element that I cherish greatly. Even though she faced many health challenges of her own, she selflessly sought my blessing and delighted in my progress. So my sorrow over her recent parting was painful but brief, for I know she is now with the King of Kings.

To Bo, friend and mentor. I value your input into my life, your insight, actions and heart's dedication spoke volumes to me about love. You always encouraged me to participate in the giftings of The Holy Spirit, which are given for the benefit of the body of Christ.

To my Professor Wilf – When my desire and passion was buried so deeply that it seemed I could not type another word you encouraged and coaxed me to go further than I had dared to dream or imagine possible. Gradually I gained the courage necessary to realize the possibilities, which included this book.

Chris, I appreciate your tenacity and attention to detail. Each chapter is better for it. Your clear thinking helped me be more succinct and, in some cases, sparked new insights. I am truly grateful for your commitment to this project, your months of hard work and, most importantly, you.

To my family and friends, thank you for your continued prayers, support and love.

Introduction

Through my extensive counseling experience, I met many who desired unconditional love but rarely received it, whether as a child or as an adult. When I decided to write about this, I was surprised by the many additional insights that followed.

I came to realize that none of us are born with a pure infilling of love. Can it be learned, cultivated, experienced or bestowed? Maybe. But I doubt it. The heart has only one hope for being satiated: our creator.

I have yet to meet an adult whose heart has not been bruised, or whose spirit has not been damaged in some way. It helps explain why everyone wants to be accepted, loved and understood. Not only at the emotional level, but at the spiritual, too. In fact, our very existence depends on knowing the love of Christ.

Eternal Love explores the many ways He is our source of life. But there is also the other side. Humanistic schools of thought, doctrines of men, those who purport truth but misrepresent and deceive, are agents of evil, enemies who try to destroy what love has sown.

That's why I encourage you to take a risk and seek out eternal love now. But, I caution, do so with the Spirit for, as scripture teaches, "Flesh gives birth to flesh, but Spirit gives birth to Spirit" (John 3: 6).

The Holy Spirit is on this earth to do God's will. He is part of the Godhead. Believers in Christ have intimacy with God through the Holy Spirit.

No amount of hoping can make it happen. It can only be initiated through our acceptance of the authentic God (the creator of the universe, the who says of himself, "I Am That I Am") as well as His Holy Spirit.

As Paul the apostle states, we must "stay the course." As King David exemplified, we must endeavor to "seek after God's own heart." Yet, all the while, we must also have a childlike faith. It's necessary because it puts us in a place to receive something from our Heavenly Father, the One who gives generously to all who are His and who ask expectantly.

In the following pages, I offer renewed hope. Regardless of where you start, no matter how difficult or advantageous your position, the reality of love divine is just the opening chapter. It is the beginning of God's blessing (which will affect your soul, mind, will and emotions) for God desires to transform every aspect of your life through His eternal love.

Chapter 1

Perspectives on Love

The topic of love has a beginning but will never have an ending. The full meaning of love is so broad, wide also deep no human mind can fathom or plumb its depths. There are moments of enlightenment where we can grasp some of meaning. At other times, meaningful insight escapes our reach. How could God, with His infinite knowledge of man's fallen state, choose love as the way to relate to His creation?

God's commitment in pursuing as well as relating to His beloved never ended. "We love because He first loved us" (1 John 4:19 ESV) Our hope is that perhaps a lifetime of searching the depth of His love may reveal more of love's true meaning. Only then can this divine deposit in our heart reveal its exhilarating truth.

To say all sources of love are from God brings forward the infinite also unfathomable dimension of the Creator. To measure the depth, height and width of God is like trying to measure the universe with all its galaxies. All the books in the world about love would not depict or fully illuminate the subject. Just when we grasp a small part of this concept the scope widens to become elusive again. The insanity of such a task would be laughable, if not foolish. Accepting the Word that we are loved unconditionally, by God Almighty, opens the screening of our heart to allow the freedom of discovery available in this heavenly love.

Through the ages many have tried to elucidate or explain the unexplainable.

"Since the beginning of time, man has tried to define and understand the meaning of love-an impossible task. Love is one of the greatest examples of the power of our heart. Our brains cannot explain or define completely the amazing power of love and yet when we are in love our hearts seem to understand it completely."[1]

Love's meaning is so broad because there can be so many expressions, insights, including experiences of this poignant passion in the heart. The heart of the Father is brought forward into the natural by sometimes-unexplained movements that defy reason. Love, like so many untouchable ideas in our lives, is left to subjectivity or relativity. The word *love* can be ambiguous and incomprehensible because of its diverse perspective, understanding or expression. But one thing is true: divine, unconditional love exists.

"If I take away the consequences of people's choices, I destroy the possibility of love. Love that is forced is no love at all."[2]

Loving gestures may include sharing a meal, a helping hand, a kind word in a difficult situation, or act of

[1] Paul Pearsall, PhD., The Heart's Code (Broadway Books, New York, NY 1999) p.175

[2] William P. Young The Shack, (Windblown Media, 4680 Calle Norte, Newbury Park, CA, 2007) p.190

kindness, such as visiting someone in the hospital, or caring for someone ill. Other gestures, such as a gift of money, speak of love. Any act of benevolence, however, is love.

"One must never be satisfied with his ability to love. No matter where he is, it is always just a beginning."[3]

The spiritual collinear or one-dimensional perspective of the Lord is indicative of the spiritual realm with its activity in the natural. Or what is happening in the unseen spiritual realm can be witnessed here in the natural. Jesus came from the spiritual realm yet while here He was fully man. He operated in the physical realm yet was fully able to see what His heavenly Father was doing. We are spirit beings having a physical and emotional experience in our bodies. Is there hope for us, His children, that we can love like He loved and follow as He followed His Father? So Jesus said to them, "Truly, truly, I say to you, the Son can do nothing of his own accord, but only what he sees the Father doing. For whatever the Father does, that the Son does likewise. For the Father loves the Son and shows him all that he himself is doing..." (John 5:19-20 ESV) His faith remained strong and secure in all of His choices and actions. Even through the most difficult times of temptation He never failed. As our intimacy develops with Jesus and the Holy Spirit we can be so in tune with Him that we can have a similar walk.

"An examination of the natural gives insight into the spiritual."[4]

The world today is in a tumultuous uproar both spiritually and naturally. Unsettling events cause a weakness

---

[3] Leo Buscaglia, PhD., Love (Ballantine Books, New York, 1972) p.130
[4] Wilfred R. Kent, The Greatest Love Story...ever told, (Promedia Printers and Publishers (Pty) Ltd., Pretoria, South Africa, 1995) p.16

within the heart because some are fear inducing and catastrophic. The questions begin with, where is God if He
loves us? Why are these terrible events happening?

Yet there is a heightened interest in spirituality. This
is evidenced by the supernatural activity taking place
around the world. Both love and hate, good and evil, have
been ramped up to levels not seen to this point in history.
The enemy of our souls is being challenged. Revivals of
faith in Jesus are like exploding brush fires burning in
many areas of the world. Civil wars and terrorism, on the
other hand, are causing unprecedented fear as people try
to survive or escape. The very thought of demons inter-
fering, influencing and controlling believers and unbelievers alike seems to many preposterous, although many
can attest to their existence both in their lives, the lives of
family and friends. The evil in the world is undeniable as
evidenced through heinous attitudes and acts. The Lord
tells us clearly the battle is not against flesh and blood but
against principalities and powers unseen. (2 Corinthians
10:3 ESV)

If that is where the genuine battle lies why is the reality of such a battle not perceived or commonly spoken of
today? What would such a work entail?

The incredible love He brought to earth is without
end. Every life path chosen in Him inevitably displays
including speaks of His love eternal. However, opposition is encountered where evil is present moreover, there
is chaos, confusion, fear, hatred including doubt. When
the Lord speaks of a new heaven and earth where peace
reigns, a likely question is what will the transition period
look like? A collision course will determine where the
battle that now rages will end. There will be a significant spiritual change witnessed in our day - to day lives

including throughout the world. The course has been set as a consequence, we may be the generation that will witness profound happenings on earth. The spiritual rousing never, through the world's history, eased or ended also will not end until Christ returns. Perhaps before He appears again we will see the dark spiritual realm eliminated in meticulous calculation through divine wisdom.

Perhaps we have not yet experienced the fullness of His love! There no doubt will be a time, when only in difficulty through testing do we fully come to understand the scope of His mighty love and the freedom we can obtain. The believers' perspectives on love change as the earth shudders and groans threatening life's circumstances. Believers often labor under the heavy oppression of the enemy. Uncertainty and doubt creep in the result that is to become hot, lukewarm or cold as their faith is tested.

"If one wishes to know love, one must live love, in action."[5]

We know with certainty the end of this incredible love story, which has at least one more chapter. This finale` or apocalypse, as stated in the book of Revelation, has yet to be played out. There are many levels of warfare in the spiritual realm. One such battle takes place daily for and within the soul of man.

On the cross by Jesus conquering sin and death this great love story is for those who believe in Him.

The journey of love is filled with twists and turns, hills and valleys but when in His care, always points to His unconditional love. It is a gift available to all but all do not accept this gift by faith.

---

[5] Leo Buscaglia, PhD., Living, Loving & Learning, (Ballantine books, New York, 1982) p.84

Jesus is purportedly speaking "McKenzie, my purposes are not for my comfort or yours. My purposes are always and only an expression of love. I purpose to work life out of death, to bring freedom out of brokenness and turn darkness into light. What you see as chaos, I see as a fractal. All things must unfold, even though it puts all those I love in the midst of a world of horrible tragedies - even the one closest to me."[6]

We know the ending of this love story, Jesus said "I have overcome the world." (John 16:33 ESV)

---

[6] William P. Young The Shack, (Windblown Media, 4680 Calle Norte, Newbury Park,CA, 2007) p.191

Chapter 2

Love Completes the Circle

Could any person who ever lived desired your ultimate good? If the answer is 'yes', then would he or she die for you? There have doubtless been a number of people who have declared their strong love, even unto death, but few if any could ever accomplish it.

Christ's death was sacrificial to save all people from judgment including eternal damnation. He did it for the supreme good of all peoples based on unconditional love.

Expressions of love may include the love for a person, place, laws, organizations, passion for the physical body, nature, food, money, higher education, power, fame, recognition..etc. Different people place varying degrees of importance on the priorities also passions they surround themselves with. Love is essentially an abstract concept, much easier to experience than to explain. Once experienced, it becomes the only reality that has any significance in life.

"To live in love is to live in life, and to live in life is to live in love."[7]

What did the creator of the world do to initiate this relationship?

Jesus Christ came as a living sacrifice freely choosing death for the atonement of sin. This ultimate act of love then transfers the decision to man securing choices through free will. The first option is to choose love along with freedom by experiencing life more abundantly. The second option is to live the self-willed worldly way. People in the latter camp experience short term delight and long term agony.

To know the delight of experiencing unconditional love by free will divinely given enhances our lives. Jesus knew the cost of dying on a cross and even experiencing the greatest suffering of taking on God's just wrath. He also knew the joy that was set before Him, the future reward. He endured based on the joy that gave Him the strength to endure. (Hebrews 12:2 ESV) Believing in Him returns us to the finished side of the cross where we can know such love. We now can experience the love that Adam and Eve took part in before sin entered the world.

The Lord Jesus desires that everyone would choose Him as Savior, to experience His love daily and to be fully submersed in His supernatural Holy Spirit activities. (John 3:8 NIV) "The wind blows wherever it pleases. You hear its sound, but you cannot tell where it comes from or where it is going. So it is with everyone born of the Spirit."

© 2011 Doreen S. Barber

---

[7] Leo Buscaglia, Living, Loving & Learning, (Ballantine Books, New York, 1982) p.84

Love screams for an even playing field of respect and
empathy.
Love crosses all social, cultural and economic borders. All
of us want to be accepted equally with our ultimate
good held in hand.
Our hearts want to be cared for by the tenderest touch.
We have the ability to love, but not all love.
We have the ability to care, but not all care.
We have compassion, but not all are compassionate.
We have wisdom, but all are not wise.
We have talents, but all are not talented.
We have access to Spirit, but not all exercise this insight.
We have insight but not all can see with their hearts.
We have intuition, but not all can intuitively see.
We can ask for growth, but not all are able to grow
We have a yearning to meet the untapped power but
unfortunately,
Not all meet the Creator.

Love is the greatest gift that anyone can receive or
offer to another because it encompasses all aspects of en-
dorsement, acceptance, and grace.

If you were asked to look down on earth from the edge
of heaven to describe what you see, what would you say?
Perhaps from heaven the person with clouded vision
would say it looks like a garbage heap that, in comparison to heaven, one would not want to visit or inhabit. The
Lord looks down with firm conviction in love. "I love and
died for this world called a garbage heap. The world is My
treasure, which I created with purpose and plan. I knit all
people together in their mother's womb. I love all people,
they are my children and I know each heart."

Jesus knowing the heart of man understands the difficulty understanding His divine question. Our lack of

godly understanding to His all knowing or wise question, would be evident by the look on His face. It would speak of the human ignorance in providential comprehension. His heart for this earth is full of compassion, understanding, grace together with love. His eyes never see a garbage heap, they see tormented souls in need of a Savior.

"No man can possibly know what life means, what the world means what anything means, until he has a child and loves it. And then the whole universe changes and nothing will ever again seem exactly as it seemed before." Lofcadio Hearn.

From His throne above the earth this world its the inhabitants is the most beautiful of all His creations.

His love comes from the heart; it is spoken from the heart, experienced in the heart, and returned, completing the circle.

Can this love be explained unless we have experienced it?

We need to know who walks with us daily moreover, who is the source of this great love. How can we give it away without knowing this absolute love, His love, for ourselves?

"Love is always bestowed as a gift - freely, willingly, and without expectation. It is offered even when not acknowledged or appreciated. We don't love to be loved, we love to love."[8]

Without His sacrifice there would be no example of pure unconditional love.

Because of this love it assists us to take the step from theory to experience.

---

[8] Leo Buscaglia, Born For Love (Ballantine Books, New York, 1992) p.245

Love is the greatest gift any of us will ever receive. It will unlock hearts, move mountains, transform nations, rulers, emperors, to break down walls and open prison doors.

© 2011 Doreen S. Barber
Love is a gift you give to people.
Love doesn't ask for a fee nor seek payment.
Love is given without strings attached.
Love willingly wants to be obedient to the Master's call.
Love embraces all character flaws and attitudes.
Love is passed to you then completes a circle back to its
    origin. The circles get larger and wider as love moves
    forward the circle expands.
Love is what everyone recognizes although not all are
    able to fully understand or reciprocate.

"For to miss love is to miss life." Thornton Wilder says, "There is a land of the living and a land of the dead, and the bridge is love. The only survival and the only meaning."[9]

Coming into the Lord's presence brings the heart assurance we are loved as well as accepted. Through experiencing this love we are capable of imitating it. This love then ought to magnify our creator, Jesus.

Love is not to be hidden in the heart but must be demonstrated outwardly by action, deeds and speech. Meeting the Lord for the first time is a very exciting time. Every color seems brighter, every person happier, every action a beautiful and fulfilling accomplishment.

---

[9] Leo Buscaglia, Ph. D., Living, Loving & Learning (Ballantine Books, New York, 1982) p.154

There is a euphoric feeling walking in the newness of meeting Him. Every step taken with Him appears brighter than the day before.

Our expectations are above what we had ever imagined. Our goals now have changed, as we want to spend the rest of our time with our beloved. To remain in this state is not natural or normal so we must renew daily. Developing a relationship with Jesus our Lord/Creator does not happen easily or by happenstance. Neither does it occur in our natural family. This is a day to day occurrence in quality time spent. As earnestly as we declare our love, change to maturation is inevitable. Day-to-day living lowers the heights that we want to aspire to in expressing our love. The realities of life bring change to that loving feeling. The accountability, including responsibility to keep the promise to love can bring a hard reality crash. The challenge is to live the declared love we have vowed to uphold before the Lord.

Life's circumstances are daily occurrences that force us to examine our heart's character before the Lord. It is here we learn our most valuable lessons in reflecting outwardly the love we have for our Savior. This circle is then complete because the relationship begins with our Lord and ends with His affirming love.

"I know in my heart that no person can love another unless he loves humanity first. The ability to sow love stems from this inner sense of feeling connected to, rather than separate from all living creatures, all of humanity and God as well."[10]

We are those children that have been brought into the Lord's family.

---

[10] Wayne W. Dyer, There's A Spiritual Solution To Every Problem, (Harper Collins,, 10 East 53rd Street, New York, N.Y. 10022, 2001) p.175

Love

Love knows no bounds, except to the heart!
Can you hear me speak?
And ask, 'Where are the marks,
To the height of eagles peak?"
Love continues to ask,
"Are you with me?"
In showers of tenderness we bask,
No notion to ask for a fee.
"What height will you take me to?"
"To what depth will we go?"
We rose up upon eagles wings and flew"
To the valleys in each row we sowed.
We've worked and played,
Through laughter and tears,
True to the heart we have stayed,
As we worked through every fear,
This force unseen and binding forever,
No greater spirit known to man,
Unconditional, unending, unmovable, and clever,
To this love I am the biggest fan.

The Lord initiates and decrees love, we participate in
a love that transcends all barriers. The glory and honor
resides in Him.

The circle of love begins with the love offered to us by
the sacrificial death of Christ. It can only be completed
when we accept by commitment this unconditional gift.
Receiving it requires that we give it back to Him in service
to the world made in His name, thus completing the circle of love.

Chapter 3

Is Love Learned, Experienced, Cultural or Spirit-Given?

L ove has no known heights, depths, or bounds. Most Christians practice love within their learned limits or experienced boundaries. The Lord however gave himself in an unconditional, incalculably, sacrificial way by dying an innocent death so that we may truly live beyond the natural. That is the Good News of the Gospel message, the invitation, that has been offered since resurrection.

Cultural acts of doing for our fellow beings such as demonstrative kindness, compassion, empathy along with benevolence express love in a tangible manner. The Lord said giving one of these "little" (less prominent among us) ones a cup of cold water because he is a disciple will receive his reward. (Matt. 10:42 ESV) Often leadership focuses on more prominent people in the community forgetting the needs of the inconspicuous. The outward appearance of a believer often does not demonstrate the unconditional love of Jesus that edifies the heart. Gifts given by the Holy Spirit have not matured or recognized to their potential.

The word love has many different expressions from something that gives pleasure like 'I loved that meal' to one who would die for acts of patriotism. It can describe an intense feeling of affection, caring, or altruistic behavior. However, it usually refers to interpersonal love. Probably due to its psychological connection, love is one of the most common themes in art along with music.

Love has no religious regulation attached to it. Religious trappings, like judgment, tend to snare love within our heart to hold it captive. This pietism in relationships, crushes openness in like manner vulnerability. Religiosity or following demanding laws or rituals, hampers the genuine flow of compatibility, acceptance, a deeper grace that brings oneness to people.

Jesus has loved man categorically regardless of the emotional, spiritual, or the physical state. We have the same opportunity, basking in His limitless amount of love, to take it forward. Often we do not have the opportunity to develop this potential due to misguided beliefs. The potential can be more fully realized but it requires devotion to Jesus, meditating, listening prayer, searching the scriptures, allowing the Holy Spirit to make necessary erroneous mind corrections and alterations.

Growing in love is incontestable that results in genuine joy, peace, patience, kindness, goodness, faithfulness, gentleness, self-control.. etc..(Galatians 5:22) The result becomes evident in our lives. The Lord wants to teach us the import of His love besides He does this in an infinite number of ways.

Can love and tending be shown in the way animals behave?

Although this could be debated, for an animal lover the answer is 'yes'. Here is a story that demonstrates the affection of some for cats, as related by the CEO of a Health Care Facility. The Health Care Facility brought in animals of all sorts to help the in-care patients love and respond. There were cats, dogs, parrots, fish etc. The cat in this account, would bring a sense of belonging, when a patient was near death by jumping up onto their bed and staying there until the patient expired. After the person died, the cat jumped off the bed, vomited and hid for three to four days. The cat reappeared then repeated the whole process again when the next patient was near death. The dying patient was comforted and felt the closeness of this pet. This demonstrates affectionate and caring by or in the animal kingdom.

"The researchers found that those with the fewest social contacts had a death rate two and a half times higher than those who had the most social contacts. Those who have pets live longer after heart attacks than those who don't and nearly everyone knows someone who has postponed death until after Christmas, a reunion, or a birthday."[11]

We also learn to love through the people in our close proximity. If love is not demonstrated we learn indifference, disassociation likewise discontent. Criticism is judgment in disguise. Those unwilling to offer acceptance by grace have difficulty loving.

Children learn what they live. Family dynamics greatly influence a child's understanding of God's character. These early impressions further propel them along a path of faith or unbelief. Home is where the first learned references mark the our understanding of God's love. We

---

[11] Bernie S. Siegel,. M.,D., Love, Medicine & Miracles, (Harper & Row, 10 East 53rd Street, New York, N.Y. 10022, 1986) p,186-187.

embrace or reject Him based upon the undeveloped cognitive reasoning.

"The highest promise of God proceeds from the highest love."[12]

If we allow our intellect to analyze love we will always commit intellectual suicide. The mind has the ability to dictate and overrule our hearts. Vulnerability and trust will never be a part of the decision to seek love.

"The brain/body covenant is one designed primarily for staying alive, seeking stimulation, doing, and getting. In effect, the brain 'drags' your body with it to do its bidding, hauling you and your heart along on its rough ride, whether or not you are sure 'in your heart' that you want to go where it is taking you."[13]

The opposite of love is hate or perhaps indifference. When we are experiencing hate we are aware of the revulsion plus disgust someone has toward us. Our emotions are intensely aware of the abhorrence aimed in our direction further our alert buttons get pushed. Decisions at this point have to be made, how do we react with love?

Love is a belief or impression felt in the depth of our souls, which move us to new realms in the kingdom's work. Living water, life flowing from a new heart. Our hearts are trained progressively by the Spirit to be aware of His movements, being carried forward to good works. (John 3:5-8) In a relationship of love the constant is contact. This describes love Spirit inspired.

---

[12] Neale Donald Walsch, Conversations with God, (Penguin Putnam Inc, 375 Hudson Street, New York, N.Y. 10014, 1995) p.44

[13] Paul Pearsall, Ph. D., The Heart's Code, The Heart's Code (Broadway Books,New York, NY 1999) p.24

"If you could wrap every thought in love, if you could love everything and everyone, your life would be transformed."[14]

The 2006 Noble Peace Prize Winner Dr. Muhammad Yunus gives insight into the power of friendship and love. Dr. Yunus, a professor of economics lives in Bangladesh. He was perplexed by the poverty that surrounded him. He said, "I teach a series on economics but people are going hungry." One day as he walked among the people of a local village he pondered how he could help one person for one day. He soon learned that moneylenders held the people in bondage. Of forty-three people he interviewed, all baskets weavers, he found that all that was required to set them free from debt was $27.00 Moved by their need he gave each individual the amount they needed to pay off their debts. He then offered to give each of them loans to start their own business ventures with nothing held as collateral and thus the Gramine Bank was formed. Some of the businesses that were started involved raising sheep, cows, chickens, weaving baskets including selling cell phones. From that humble beginning the bank has now lent over 6 billion dollars worldwide. Fifty-eight percent of the individuals who have applied for loans are now independent business owners who are able to fully support themselves by having gotten out of poverty. Almost all of his customers are women; their children are well fed, exceeding either in school, college or university. Dr. Yunus's gesture of friendship in conjunction with feelings of compassion has forever changed the lives of those who received the opportunity to better themselves including the lives of their families. The practical

---

[14] James Ray, The Secret, (Beyond Words, 20827 N.W. Cornell Road, Suite 500, Hillsboro, Oregon, 97124-9808, 2006) p.38

teaching of Dr. Muhammad Yunus expresses love paid
forward, cultural changes necessary which likely inspired
the work of love by God's Spirit. He changed a culture that
will influence future generations.

This supernatural love can be learned as we listen
through obedience the Holy Spirit's teaching. This personal relationship is divinely given and intimately available to all people. Our purpose and calling throughout
life is to do His will through intimacy by learning to hear
His voice.

For some believers this may be a difficult concept.
The possibility of performing every charitable act under
His directive seems out of reach. The prospect, or even
the remote possibility, of attaining such a goal only exists
through the empowering of Holy Spirit. The Spirit within
us can cause us to act not from religious duty, bound by
obligations, but from divine inspiration.

Learned or cultural acts can be transitioned into genuine heart Holy Spirit love.

Love is at times learned, cultural or experienced but
the greatest of these is Holy Spirit life- breathed. "It is the
Spirit who gives life, the flesh is no help at all. The words
that I have spoken to you are spirit and life" (John 6:63,
64 ESV) His desire is that we be Elysian based rather than
acting as a result of learned behavior, social, experimen-
tal or functionary acts. As we recognize the voice of the
Lord, understand the great love that has been given, the
Spirit's work in our heart will lead us to more experiences
in genuine active Spirit love. The result is then obedience
to Him rather than self directed will. Love is a language of
the Spirit transposing itself over the 'my spirit' attitude.

We are not capable of loving as He loved without the Holy Spirit being our Helper, Spirit of Truth, and Comforter. (John 14: 16, 17, 26 ESV)

In Romans 12:9 Paul calls us to a genuine love, to abhor what is evil, to hold fast to what is good, and to love one another with brotherly affection. Holy Spirit will guide us into indisputable acts of love. To love the discards, love those who seek to harm, in addition speak all manner of evil against us.

"Mysteries cannot be grasped by intellectual prowess. Regardless of your astute intellectual powers of reason and discernment, you will never understand a mystery unless it is revealed to you by God's Spirit."[15]

Examples we have today of unselfishly giving their lives away are Mother Theresa and Heidi Baker. They work by the Holy Spirit's direction, spiritual gifts active in demonstrating miracles in the Kingdom of God. Many others are working in the fields of life as Holy Spirit anoints likewise directs these unsung heroes. Their loving acts are unexplainable to the world but speak of the Spirit within.

---

[15] Dr. Wilfred R. Kent, The Greatest Love Story..ever told, (TWM International Publishers, P.O. Box 1000, Parker, Colorado, 80134, 1995) p.2

Chapter 4

Relationship

It is hard to love anyone, even the Lord, without having a genuine relationship. Believers can be very grateful for their salvation but not have a deep personal friendship with the Lord. In kinship we understand more of Him and His love for us. The more we know Him the more we know ourselves.

If we once understood the great desire that God has for us to know Him through a relationship with His son Jesus, we would never again question why He was sent to earth. Besides salvation another great gift is the invitation to be in fellowship with Him. The amazing part of this involvement is that it never expires. The pledge given by the King of Kings is not dependent on our merits, never ceases, as the promise is established for eternity.

From our earliest moments until death, our lives are intertwined with various types and styles of relationship. From birth to death, interpersonal contact is imperative to our survival mentally, emotionally, physically and spiritually. Our bodies and souls have been created for interaction. Without relationships growth is hampered. If non-existent, we can perish. Even secular studies have shown children in orphanages who are not tenderly touched, held and caressed have a high mortality rate.

Relationships are like a finely tended garden. Gardens require the elements of water, nutrients, and sunshine to produce good fruit. Likewise, we need to be in constant contact, communicating with Holy Spirit, listening to His voice and then following His given direction. Learning to trust as we at times walk an unknown path that He has chosen for us.

Trust in any relationship necessitates time. Experience, growth and maturity teach us to trust Him to be assured He will never be unfaithful or leave us alone. Experience will always prove His word true. He is patient and kind allowing growth to maturity that will change us into the wholeness of His character.

John Fenn on a CD titled Activating Your 5 Spiritual Senses claims that Jesus told him, "I gifted everyone for what they would need according to life so that every person would totally depend on Me 100% for the challenges in life. In that everyone is equal." These are comforting words in which we can take solace when facing difficult challenges.

Every relationship, if it is to be nourished, requires quality time, respect, one-on-one interaction, besides attentive listening. As we spend time with people, our Lord, understanding, acceptance and increase intimacy. Without time together the distance between parties starts to wane. The relationship becomes stale loosing its once captivating appeal.

Keeping in touch with our friends and family brings a new awareness of what is taking place in their lives. The Bible gives the example of a prodigal son. The relationship with the younger son was broken causing emotional stress. He left his father in rebellion squandering his money in reckless living distancing himself from his family. The scripture clearly states the father loved both of his sons. Later the wayward son came to his senses repented and reunited with his father. (Luke 15:11)

The full glory of His love is only discovered through active growth in our heart. This change is evident, therefore witnessed rather than declared through the hypothesis of theory only. There is a vast difference between supposition and the reality of practical expression. When we put 'loving' into a human relationship we get a combination that invites us into a faithful union of trust.

Charice, a three-year-old witnessed her father attempting to strangle her mother. After loud screams her mother was rescued from the assault by neighbors. She never saw her father again.

When Charice was four, her mother heard singing from another room and thought it was Celine Dionne on the radio. She soon discovered it was her daughter singing and decided to have her sing at local venues. Charice dreamed big. Charice and her career were launched after attending hometown gigs and a posting on U Tube. She drew pictures and prayed to God that her wishes would come true. The pictures she drew depicted her singing with Andrea Bocelli, Celine Dionne, David Foster and Josh Groban. She began singing with these world-renowned entertainers in 2008. Her engagements will extend indefinitely. She simply says, "now I am singing for my Mom. I don't think about what happened." Her story is one of triumph over adversity.

Graham Cook states it well: "Love is a verb attached to your will. Love is always an act or action."

Jesus draws us to his heart. His love is a love that so captures us that nothing else in this world will satisfy. When the intensity of love within reaches depths and heights unexplainable, the passion of our heart is then to serve Him. Nothing else will satisfy the longing with a desire within needing expression. Our heart pants to demonstrate His love.

The relationship Jesus has with His heavenly Father is offered to us on earth. He invites us to know Him in the same manner with the identical intensity. Our earthly human minds have difficulty grasping such an idea. How could the ruler of the universe bring us mortals into a never ending union?

"Jesus wanted us to be very clear about who his Father is because we only grow in him to the degree that we trust his love for us."[16]

There is absolutely nothing we can do to justify ourselves before Jesus. Good works ritualized to gain His favor in acceptance would again put us under the law, but we "are justified by his grace as a gift, through the redemption that is in Christ Jesus" (Romans 3:24 ESV) Through salvation we are granted free, unrestricted access to Him and a love follows without fear of judgment.

---

[16] Wayne Jacobsen, He Loves Me, (Newbury Park, CA, 2007) p.37

Chapter 5

The Heart is a Lonely Hunter

The soul is the seat of our mind, our will and emotions. It is the center for life's decisions and attitudes. The soul/heart was created with a spiritual void that requires love to meet its longing and the cry from deep within. This void is unfathomable and cannot be replaced by anything other than the divine love of the Lord, who is creator of life. The heart longs to be fulfilled and to reach its designed purpose. Sadly because the heart is a lonely hunter the search never ceases until it has spiritual fulfillment. For some, the act of seeking spiritual fulfillment will lead them into the dark side with its negative promises causing ultimate upheaval, erroneous paths or destruction.

A popular country and western song states that we are looking for love in all the wrong places. Regrettably teenagers, who do not understand their misleading emotions, will often succumb to experiences that cause harm and cause chaos well into adulthood. This is the point where Biblical-based intervention, the gift of the Holy Spirit, and Christian counseling become fundamental. (Psalm 107:9

ESV) "For he satisfies the longing soul, and the hungry soul he fills with good things."

Childhood can teach us that the things done by people who say that they love us are not always good, fair, or noble. Since as children will look for and expect truth to be demonstrated by the people in their surrounding sphere, disappointment is inevitable and absolute. When children or adults are emotionally wounded in any fashion, love is kicked down the road like a can because this disappointment does not line up with their desires, wants or needs. At such points in life, one natural response is to blame or hold God accountable for His inadequacies, lack of care or attention.

"You are today where you thoughts have brought you; you will be tomorrow where your thoughts take you." James Allen

The results of our actions are expressed by our achievements and failures, societal positions and shortcomings. In all likelihood, these stations in life are influenced, patterned and modeled from the adults we watched and mimicked as children. All that we experience as children is held for future reference as we analyze our surroundings and the people in our lives. To this point behavioral analysis informs us that children are either nurtured in loving, caring and protective homes or mistreated in abusive ones.

At the core of every human being love is desired. It is an absolute prerequisite of a happy well-adjusted life. This deep innate desire is built into our DNA and will cause a deep hunger or longing for spiritual encounter. All people were created to know the divinity of God our Creator.

How we challenge life and deal with our realities in love from a heart perspective depends on many circumstantial consequences related to each individual. We are a broken and heart sick people, and this taints our views and expressions.

Life causes many disappointments and difficulties all too numerous to work through on our own. Difficult situations we face as adults may be created in childhood by emotional upheaval. These past experiences need restoration and healing. Often it is here, belief in God, His existence, that He is love encounters unbelief. Jesus has a list of approaches, encompassing endless possibilities of circumstances to bring about healing to our souls or minds, wills, and emotions. The infinity of His designs to bring change within us would fill many volumes from here to eternity. But we are only able to deal with our inner-person problems in small bits and pieces. So through the grace of our Lord, He measures and proportions each encounter perfectly.

"We believe that part of the reason the attention association area is activated during spiritual practices such as meditation is because it is heavily involved in emotional responses—and religious experiences are usually highly emotional."[17]

The ability to love is inherent in all human beings, regardless of cultures or life styles. However in many societies, the focus on idol worship or occult practices such as voodoo will result in glaring differences in how it is expressed. People there succumb to profound emotional

---

[17] Andrew Newberg, M.D., Eugene D'Aquilli, M.D., Ph.D., And Vince Rause, Why God Won't Go Away, (Dimension Books, Inc., De Bazuin, Holland, 1975) p.31

responses that take them into mind-body transformed states that are the negation of love.

"This is true because love is not love if it can be programmed. Love cannot be legislated, manipulated or litigated. It cannot be coerced or demanded. Love can only be received when it is willingly given."[18]

It is that fact which makes sense of the creation story.

Earthly pleasures do not bring the benefit or satisfaction we seek. However, our efforts to replace them with the authentic article can be as sensible as going to Antarctica when you would rather go to Hawaii. Often love so needs to be expressed that it will be lavished upon objects, hobbies, employment, social or environmental causes – objects that we give our attention to but that fulfill us for only a brief moment. The connection formed will touch the emotional realm temporarily, but it fades quickly.

The thirst for love can be described as a profound crevasse in our lives, one that cannot be filled by anything other than the divine indwelling of Jesus, the creator of all life.

He alone gives people the true fullness of love. As creator He designed us unfulfilled without His love; but when in it, to be complete and satiated. The heart is truly a lonely hunter, searching all avenues but with an outstanding lack of success. Religious activities can be just as misleading as indulging in all other manner of pleasure. Satisfaction is brief, but then the hunger and thirst begin again. Radical groups of concerned citizens will often form around some cause but just as quickly will drift apart to join new causes. We, as a people of faith,

---

[18] Wilfred R. Kent, The Greatest Love Story ...ever told, (Promedia Printers and Publishers (Pty) Ltd., Pretoria, South Africa, 1995) p.38

can bring the same passion for doing the work of Jesus but watch it ebb and flow when faced with opposition. Sometimes the security of life eternal lulls the participant into standing on the side lines instead of running the race.

(Corinthians 13:13 ESV) states "So now faith, hope, and love abide, these three; the greatest of these is love." Jesus said that love was the only element in the entire universe that was worth searching for. At the beginning of the next verse we are told to 'pursue love.' This implies that we are to seek love with passion, fervor, obsession, and enthusiasm. The lonely heart needs to hunt for love with the dedication of those followers of Jesus who never allow the search to die. Complacency is not welcome. As a believing people, where complacency is not welcome the desire and hunger grows. The quest should never stall out or end but should always be increasing.

We cannot risk becoming self-satisfied or resting from plumbing the depths of His infinite love. For those who search, there is always even deeper, more immeasurable love awaiting us.

"You are designed for love; that is part of the human architecture...In fact, it is about becoming more of who you were truly meant to be. Ultimately, it is about the authentic part of you that God created."[19]

The lonely heart is crying out for rest and peace, a peace that can only be met by the genuine love of the Heavenly Father-Jesus.

---

[19] Dr. John Townsend, Loving People (Nelson Thomas, Nashville Tennessee, 2007) p.13

Chapter 6

Expressions of Love

The Bible references three Greek words for love - Eros; Phileo; and Agapao. The p*hilia* and *agapae* words can refer to affection for someone or something. *Philia* love is based on mutual admiration. *Agape* love is selfless, with no strings attached. It is given without an expected return. *Agape* can indicate and operate in the personal and the spiritual sides of life. *Agape* love is of God and from God. God's *agape* love is demonstrated through the gift of His Son.

"In this is love, not that we have loved God but that he loved us and sent his Son to be the propitiation for our sins." (1 John 4:10 ESV)

Here is a true story of a gal who came from Africa on a dream that America offered to fulfill. Her mother saved very diligently to send her to America, a foreign country without family. After college she wanted to go to Columbia University but was unable to qualify for loans because she was not a citizen. Feeling alone in New York and desperate she searched for answers. On a park bench sat a couple with a sign that read; "Talk to Me." After listening to her story a couple advised her to get a stand and list details of her dream. They recognized that she was brilliant, and that she was searching to fulfill her dream. She took their advice and stood in front of a downtown office building six and one-half hours each day looking for someone to help her with a loan. A black woman who was late for a meeting stopped and talked to her. Looking at the scholastic marks she had achieved this lady offered to help. She raised the money by speaking to her friends, which caused a multiplication effect. The money raised totaled $40,000, and came in from all over America. She is now in her second year and yes, she is brilliant. She also became a member of this black woman's family as well as numbered among her friends. This is what is meant by *agape* love.

"Love is always the right thing to do. Both culture and Scripture attest that all moral absolutes can be reduced to one: To love is always right; not to love is always wrong."[20]

Friendship and love can be likened to a flowering plant that when watered, fertilized and exposed to adequate sunshine brings forth beauty with a sweet fragrance that lifts the spirit of those who come into its presence.

The side of Jesus who overturns tables leaves us questioning the tough side of love. (John 2:13-17) He verbally confronts hypocrites (Matt. 23) He disciples those he loves and chastises every son whom he receives. (Heb. 12:6)

There are many circumstances in life that seem harsh and require tough-minded love in action. The truth is love never fails. Areas in our lives that need corrective measures in our relationship with Jesus always fall on our

---

[20] Josh McDowell and Norm Geisler, Love Is Always Right (Word Publishing, Dallas Texas, 1996) p.33

side of the ledger; not on His. We are being made into His perfect likeness; not the reverse. Only the Lord himself can judge the true motive of the heart. We are responsible for our own accountability before Him. Love in its purest form comes from the Spirit and is represented through the actions of the individual. Believers disappoint in their actions with others and the reasons for this have multiple facets. The actions are something that should not be judged strictly by outward observation. We are prone to make quick unsubstantiated judgments. Restoring the individual is brought about through personal contact, counseling, prayer and seeking the Lord.

"All of your conflicts with others are never between you and them; they are between you and God."[21]

The Lord has shown people the way to love. Some embrace it others don't. How many? Jesus lost one of His disciples and a third of the angels to hell. He loves the world but many of His created will also be lost to the everlasting torment of hell. The Lord does not change His position to suit His creation. We have free-will with its choices and consequences, but His love is ever being offered at no cost to us. It is freely given.

This is a most profound time in history where we are witnessing many miraculous occurrences of God. His love is being poured out in great measure. The spirit world both good and evil has been ramped up. As the darkness of this world increases, the love and grace of Jesus is also magnifying throughout the earth.

Love comes in many forms from the smallest grain of sand to the largest bolder. All answers lie within Him.

---

[21] Wayne W. Dyer, There's A Spiritual Solution To Every Problem,(Harper Collins, 10 East 53rd Street, New York, N.Y.10022, 2001) p.196

Jesus states "For everyone who asks receives, and the one who seeks finds, and to the one who knocks it will be opened." (Matt. 7:8 ESV)

The Holy Ghost sometimes whispers, and sometimes shouts; regardless He is always active. The Church is often lacking ears to hear and upon hearing is slow to respond. We can be a people of indifference not interested in pursuing all that has been made available to us.

"Doctors don't know everything really. They understand matter, not spirit. And you and I love in the spirit." William Sarovan, The Human Comedy.

Life (Love) is about how to - *Dance in the Rain*

"It was a busy morning, about 8:30, when an elderly gentleman in his 80's, arrived to have stitches removed from his thumb. He said he was in a hurry as he had an appointment at 9:00 am.

I took his vital signs and had him take a seat, knowing it would be over an hour before someone would be able to see him.

I saw him looking at his watch and decided, since I was not busy with another patient, I would evaluate his wound.

On exam, it was well healed, so I talked to one of the doctors, got the needed supplies to remove his sutures and redress his wound.

While taking care of his wound, I asked him if he had another doctor's appointment this morning, as he was in such a hurry. The gentleman told me no, that he needed to go to the nursing home to eat breakfast with his wife.

I inquired as to her health. He told me that she had been there for a while and that she was a victim of Alzheimer's Disease. As we talked, I asked if she would be upset if he was a bit late. He replied that she no longer knew who he was, that she had not recognized him in five years now.

I was surprised, and asked him, "And you still go every morning, even though she doesn't know who you are?"

He smiled as he patted my hand and said, "She doesn't know me, but I still know who she is." I had to hold back tears as he left. I had goose bumps on my arm, and thought,

That is the kind of love I want in my life. True love is neither physical nor romantic. True love is an acceptance of all that is, has been, will be and will not be.

The happiest people don't necessarily have the best of everything; they just make the best of everything they have. Life isn't about how to survive the storm, but how to dance in the rain." Author Unknown

A heart warming story of love given and unrecognized by the recipient. A statement of *agape* love.

"Deterrents to love are man-made. Love will not be deterred. Love flows like a river; always itself, yet ever changing, recognizing no obstacle.."[22]

The discovery of *agape* or divine love surpasses all that we could have imagined or hoped to experience in genuine unconditional love. *Agape,* with as its author, Jesus allows us to partner in expression of unconditional love reaching the most exhilarating heights. Expressions of love freely given (*agape)* acknowledge the highest good for an individual.

---

[22] Leo Buscaglia, Love (Ballantine Books, 1972) p.131

Chapter 7

Love Brought Forward Into Human Terms

Jesus, the King of Kings in human form, who willingly left heaven to come to earth, has allowed us to witness a glimpse of heaven's reality. He is now walking among us daily, speaking by His Spirit, always deeply committed and demonstrating divine love. This love is like no other love in the universe, freely given to those who will receive Him. What manner of love is this?

This love goes beyond our belief, teaching or doctrinal system. This system of God given love is operational whether it is in a church setting, an educational institute, an informal gathering with friends, a political convention, or in the sanitation department.

A set of guidelines, goals, teachings, or values all have a basic structure to them with many variables added to the mix. The populace at large is influenced, guided and directed to live life within such boundaries. However the spiritual side of people often has no concrete or substantial anchor to hold to. People are tossed around like leaves in the wind. They blow from one updraft to the next before landing. Unfortunately many never find authentic unconditional love. On the other hand, we know God is capable of intersecting into lives at any given moment, personally confronting the individual. Consequentially, change is always guaranteed.

"The wind blows where it wishes, and you hear its sound, but you do not know where it comes from or where it goes. So it is with everyone who is born of the Spirit." (John 3:8 ESV)

Our lives, to be effective, must be informed by the supernatural/spiritual presence of Jesus. If we accept Jesus and adhere to the faith, our resolve to be true-heart-ed followers will be set in stone. Our decisions and practices will shape the actions of our families reaching forward through many generations. We will hold a set of beliefs, philosophical doctrine, and persuasions that project love, and these will play out in earthly realities.

"There is a God who can only be experienced by going beyond experience."[23]

Love knows no heights or depths. It is a solid truth that has no perimeters. Love is able to say, 'I do not agree with what you say, although I take notice of your opinion and respect your conviction.' As we become secure in our own beliefs, our increasing sense of freedom and grace will allow others the same privilege. It is not to us to judge a soul's eternal placement. "And when He (Holy Spirit) comes, He will convict the world concerning sin and righteousness and judgment: concerning sin because they do not believe in Me." (John 16:8-9 ESV)

The opinions held by different believers are neither right nor wrong in and of themselves. We in the Christian community are often quick to cast aside others who do

---

[23] Deepak Chopra, How To Know God (Three Rivers Press, New York, New York, 2000) p.158

not have the same set of beliefs as us, with criticisms being leveled under the guise of love. That is to miss the point. The commonality of faith is receiving Jesus as our Savior. Doctrinal issues will never be agreed upon this side of heaven, and in heaven the arguments of past years will hold no meaning or substance in the light of His glory.

In reality the world is deficient of love, but in the church there is misguided expectation that people will automatically love their neighbor as they are commanded to. All too frequently the actual attitude conveyed is - if you think like I do then I will accept you; if you act a certain way that I approve of, then I will love you; if you speak a certain way I will embrace you; or if you believe as I do I will befriend you. This is not the model Jesus left us to follow. Love necessitates no hooks or controls, demands, or expectations. Therefore the thoughts, attitudes and heart values we propagate in life today require scrutiny by His divine power. We all need to guard against judging others.

"When you judge another person you do not define them. You merely define yourself as someone who needs to judge."[24]

Judgmental attitudes are insidious as they creep into daily life. We need to remember that this world was created by a loving God who states in (John 8:16 ONM) "... my judgment is true." Under the Old Testament law every person was to judge only him or herself.

When love is operating at its highest level, faith in Jesus as Savior can be proclaimed without fear. When harshly judged, we need not take it as a personal slight

---

[24] Wayne W. Dyer, There's A Spiritual Solution To Every Problem (Harper Collins,, 10 East 53rd Street, New York, N.Y. 10022, 2001) p.133

or offense but offer grace and forgiveness, trusting Holy Spirit to bring the healing we need and desire. Our response is to offer love even though it may be a difficult process. In difficult times, there is less likelihood of being completely understood by our fellow parishioners. Regardless of where we find ourselves, we are still His children whom He looks on with satisfaction and delight. What really matters is our heart's position with the Lord, and there is also comfort in that there will always be those who always stand with us in support, prayer and protection. Being blessed by that same grace that God has so lavishly bestowed on us all, we each need to see the potential in others through 'grace-healed eyes.'

"To love a person," said Dostoevsky, "means to see him as God intended him to be."[25]

As people, we generally want to be heard, understood and accepted just as we are. But the Lord loves us far too much to tolerate such self-satisfaction.

One insight gathered is that divine Godly love from His heart, when deposited into ours, is then experienced and spoken as unconditional love.

Love on this earth may be determined by conditions placed upon it. The behavior and actions of an individual can determine most relationships. In the purest form of love the criteria should not hurt, harm or disrespect. Unfortunately it can be hampered and lost through unbecoming behaviors that cause wounding to others.

Our characters must be developed in order to fulfill love. This process involves many areas of our lives including change from within, developing our qualities and gifting, growth and maturity, but the fruit of the Spirit

---

[25] Philip Yancey, What's So Amazing About Grace? (Zondervan Publishing House, Grand Rapids, Michigan 49530, 1997) p. 159

is love, hope, peace, long suffering, patience, goodness, faithfulness, gentleness, self-control, and joy is available to us all.

"This is the point: growth develops the capacity to love."[26]

And it is at these points in life that Holy Spirit is always available to take us further in the process.

Love is a non-inherited commodity. Some would like to believe it can be transmitted through our genealogy. Lifestyles and beliefs can be witnessed, impressions influencing, which then may be transferred forward. This is an individual walk face to face with Jesus. Jesus suffered disgrace, disrespect, shame, abandonment and rejection to accomplish the ultimate good for us. Along with the mental torment came the physical abuse and death. This unconditional love He was asked to bring through His free will and individualized death. Jesus instituted unconditional love as He consensually placed Himself on the cross having accepted that requirement from the foundation of the earth. His obedience brought eternal life with more abundant life promised to us, His children, on this earth. He showed us His humanity as He walked this earth exuding great wisdom, compassion, empathy, healing and love.

If we accept such a gift and act on it; love begins to alter us from within. It is the most powerful force on earth brought by this man, Jesus. There is an unseen transformation of our soul into the spiritual likeness of Him.

Living inside love's verbal and non-verbal communication and physical movements is an expression of love's

---

[26] Dr. John Townsend, Loving People (Thomas Nelson, Nashville Tennessee, 2007) p.25

true integrating work. It is like an art form flowing, moving, dancing and creating.

Before the world recognized Him as Savior the three years of His ministry turned the known world into disarray. This human Jesus called Himself God and demonstrated love, power, grace and wisdom unseen to that point in history.

Who can fathom such a gift that has cost us nothing, with no prerequisite but to have embraced and accepted such a gift?

We were fashioned to be actively partnering with Jesus who came forward as divine to the deprived human condition.

The Lord God premeditated by purpose that we, as humans need to express our existence through love, just as Christ showed us the path to love by His life.

Chapter 8

Love: Spirit Prompted

Some have likened love to faith, where it is an accepted known in religion. Perhaps to others it is a feeling of emotion justified as a state of being. Some would say it encompasses all of these areas. However to describe love as only an emotion or faith would have connotations of only participating in loving acts as our feelings lead us, a belief that one holds tightly to but never exhibits openly. Faith in action may have the result in moving ahead spontaneously without any emotional attachment.

Jesus has perfectly placed the Holy Spirit as our supporter and Spirit of Truth here with us until we either enter eternity or until He appears again on earth. In either way His great love is in action.

(James) speaks in (2:18, 20 ESV) But someone will say, "You have faith and I have works." Show me your faith apart from your works, and I will show you my faith by my works.

(v.20) "Do you want to be shown you foolish person, that faith apart from works is useless?" Love requires an action.

A kind but indiscriminate action could be one of the
greatest gifts recipients have ever received, although perhaps not what the Lord had intended for their growth.
Often we rush into situations believing we know what the
Lord is doing and are set back or fail miserably. Wisdom
and direction from the Spirit of God is a fundamental
key to everything we do. Progressing in the Spirit life en-
ables us to be more aware and in-tune to His wishes and
directives.

"I can relax and remember that the spirit is God,
which is synonymous with love."[27]

The Spirit is alive and working but too often 'knowing
Him' is based on many incorrect avenues of learning. We
are exposed to and influenced by Bible teachers, parents,
and the culture we live in likewise our surroundings with
tragic or negative experiences. Conclusions are based on
outside influences, at times inaccurately. The knowing
that Jesus had with His Father is our desired relationship.
Scripture, personal experiential knowledge validated by
Scripture, and listening to His direction are the valued
intimate path for us to follow. For a number in the body
of Christ there is an indolent approach to exploring the
miraculous. It is viewed as inconsequential to their belief
system or of no present relevancy. However despite the
evidence of both scripture and experience many dismiss
signs and wonders as unknown since the passing of the
Apostles. The evidence of the supernatural however is
compelling and available. Jesus incontestably and com-
passionately displayed His love and power in our time.

---

[27] Wayne W. Dyer, There's A Spiritual Solution To Every Problem
(Harper Collins,, 10 East 53rd Street, New York, N.Y. 10022, 2001) p.11

"This wide distribution of gifts across the body of Christ is what Joel prophesied when he saw the Holy Spirit coming on all people in the last days (Joel 2:28-29)[28]"

Never the less there is mostly a polite nod given to miracles and healing present today. Many people sit on the sidelines non-committed either way.

The electronic age is breeding a society of fast action, gratification in the moment. Few are spending time in the thought provoking encounters about eternity or the life changing miracles of today. Following the crowd mentality has always been a part of society. At some point in life the hard and difficult questions require a personalized answer.

If God is acknowledged as Creator then where is the Holy Spirit today? Is He active, alive and working in this world?

For many the mention of 'Holy Spirit' sends people on an emotional roller coaster titled 'fear.' This seems to trigger memories of negative occurrences in their lives that often are not associated with anything but unbelief. Some how God and Jesus stand alone and the 'Spirit' doesn't belong in the grouping. Perhaps this is because Scripture is not taken seriously or there is failed understanding as to His role in the Trinity.

"We all like to think that we are purely reasonable and objective. But the truth is, as one person has said, that we often tow our brains around behind us to justify what we already believe."[29]

---

[28] Jack Deere, Surprised By The Power Of The Spirit (Zondervan Publishing House, Grand Rapids, Michigan, 1993) p.64

[29] Jack Deere, Surprised By The Power Of The Spirit (Zondervan Publishing House, Grand Rapids, Michigan, 1993) p.45

Scripture clearly tells us who Spirit or Holy Spirit is, His attributes, His work etc... Christ knew He was leaving this world and those around him would desire to be with Him. He states where He was going Peter could not come now but would follow later. (John 13:36 ESV)

His love assured the disciples that He would not leave them alone and He told them plainly that He had little time left with them before His departure. He assured them there was a place prepared for them and He would come again and take them to Himself. Jesus knew their needs and spoke to them as a loving friend. By the nature of His character He was preparing them for their future without him leaving them as orphans. He states He is going to prepare a place for them, that their hearts are not to be troubled, that the works they will do will be greater than His, and He will give them a Helper (Holy Spirit) - Spirit of Truth to be with them forever. (John 14:16)

The realization of His departure likely caused the disciples a lot of uncertainty, fear and sorrow. Theirs was a limited understanding of events about to take place. His extraordinary love again was demonstrated by Him sending the Holy Spirit.

Jesus continues with the description of Holy Spirit and His work. (John 16:5-15 ESV)

He now has captured their attention declaring he had not told them previous to this because He was with them. He states that He will not speak on His own authority but whatever He hears He will speak. He will speak about things to come and He will glorify me (Jesus), for he will take whatever is mine and declare it to you. (John 16:14 ESV)

Key elements in this verse; Jesus only does what He sees the Father doing, nothing more or less and the Holy

Spirit will do the same. The healing ministry of Jesus was given to him at different times and in different situations. Therefore Holy Spirit today, through people, does only what He hears Jesus doing. In (Luke 24: 49, cf. Acts 1:8) "They received a special promise to be clothed with power from on high."[30] The promise given in the Greek is '*ed uow*' indicating to be clothed or covered like a garment which we sink into.

With that promise given and the events that took place after Pentecost a new era of signs and wonders began. The disciples and followers of Jesus began to demonstrate His love. The encounters we witness today of miraculous healing is the direct result of love given through Christ, now by His Spirit.

"An examination of the natural gives insight into the spiritual."[31]

"Jesus is not content to preach about the kingdom; he also demonstrates the kingdom with works of power."[32]

Today the Holy Spirit is moving and touching people under the Lord's direction. Experiences of Holy Spirit's touch are world wide with pockets of revival and movements of proclamation in Jesus name.

"Our experience determines much of what we believe and do, and often it determines much more than we are aware of or would admit."[33] This quote comes from a former Professor at the Dallas Seminary who began

[30] Jack Deere Surprised By The Power Of The Spirit (Zondervan Publishing House, Grand Rapids, Michigan, 1993) p.67
[31] Wilfred R. Kent, The Greatest Love Story...ever told. (Promedia Printers and Publishers (Pty) Ltd., Pretoria, South Africa, 1995) p.16
[32] Jack Deere, Surprised By The Power Of The Spirit (Zondervan Publishing House, Grand Rapids, Michigan, 1993) p.226
[33] Jack Deere, Surprised By The Power Of The Spirit (Zondervan Publishing House, Grand Rapids, Michigan, 1993) p.46

studying signs and wonders from a fresh new look. He also states "Over the years, I have observed that the majority of what Christians believe is not derived from their own patient and careful study of the Scriptures. The majority of Christians believe what they believe because godly and respected teachers told them it was correct."[34]

Miracles or supernatural manifestations are a normal part of witnessing His presence and power on earth. His love is demonstrated through the touch and transformations of impossible natural situations. Perhaps not believing in miracles is because exposure for most believers is rare.

On a healing mission outreach trip to Columbia I was led to a young man who had been in a horrific car accident. He sat in a wheel chair with his left leg straight out and his left arm paralyzed and limp beside him. I was led to pray for this young man by a woman who insisted I follow her. After asking Jesus to heal and waiting for a sign his paralyzed arm above the elbow began to vibrate. It had the appearance of ten thousand worms moving under the skin. After a few minutes he tried lifting his arm. Slowly at first and then with more force. I asked through an interrupter what he was feeling. He replied that he was gaining strength, something he had not felt since the accident. As we continued praying and waiting on Holy Spirit the area below his elbow started having the same movement. This continued on for another period of time. From this point on the fingers that were purple and lifeless began to get their natural color back and he slowly began to move them. At this point he tried to lift his

---

[34] Jack Deere, Surprised By The Power Of The Spirit (Zondervan Publishing House, Grand Rapids, Michigan, 1993) p.47

arm—this time he lifted it about two inches off his lap. Miraculous, yes indeed! Our God heals!

His work through Holy Spirit is alive and thriving today.

(Corinthians 16:14 ESV) "Let all that you do be done in love."

Chapter 9

Another Avenue of Love

Emotional and physical healing are extraordinary avenues of love, incontestable and available for the asking.

We as adults may have that damaged child still living within our souls. At times the child screams for attention and at other times it is walking with its head down hurt and wounded.

Not visible to the naked eye is the deep emotional pain, which is indicative of life's struggles. These dark crevices and deep valleys require the light of the Spirit of Truth. Only He can illuminate by His power, mend and restore the heart to wholeness.

Inner healing: Holy Spirit plumbs the depth of the soul to regenerate areas that keep us from the maturity we were designed to experience. Many believers have accepted His work with anticipation through this divine encounter. As this author said, "At once I had the strange sensation as if a dimmer switch had turned the inside of my entire body to maximum power." [35] This power is so

---

[35] Eckhart Tolle....A New Earth (Penguin Group, 375 Hudson Street, New York, 2005)p.175

incredible that it is undeniable yet incomprehensible in understood verbiage.

The term 'inner healing' has been in practice for many years. It relates to the work of Holy Spirit in exorcism, deep emotional, physical healing, divine revelations and encounters. Although most of these manifestations are attributed to Holy Spirit likely some are importers and counterfeit. Spiritual discernment is required.

Outward behavior is unequivocal as appearances and attitude is evidenced by actions. The body language and unpleasant verbal activity of angry or upset people speaks volumes. A person who suddenly demonstrates an outburst of displeasure over what appears to be a minor occurrences may also be demonstrating inward emotional hurt, trauma, abuse, offense or injury. These types of outbursts may be helped by 'inner healing.'

Pastor John Wimber pioneered a movement that led to a sweeping awareness of deep intimacy with Holy Spirit resulting in changed hearts. These changes brought a deeper love for Jesus. Many thousands if not hundreds of thousands became hungry and passionate to know Him more fully. Inviting Jesus to transcend deep into their hearts led to life altering occurrences. Another couple of pioneers in 'inner healing' were John and Paula Sanford who have written many books and hosted schools where deep painful memories surfaced, and hurtful experiences were wiped clean.

Sometimes our spiritual awareness is very limited in the area of emotional healing. Many people suffer in silence by coping in their wounded state. There is no framework for what is available through Holy Spirit's power because many denominations do not bring this forward through teaching. He is the Helper that all too often is not called upon to assist or asked to lead.

Some of our hurts get layered as we walk on life's journey. Our deep pain, sometimes unrecognized, may have destructive effects on those around us in addition to its toxic effect in ourselves. As the layers increase so does the tension in our sensitivities, which niggle us for resolution. The Holy Spirit is responsible for drawing our thoughts to these areas, although He is not often recognized as the source. This awareness requires a response in His direction for help to bring the necessary healing. Jesus is always available but for most He is the last resort.

This healing occurs deep within our souls influencing our mind will and emotions. This healing touch unknown may or may not involve any actions or words, just the deep presence of the Holy Spirit. Jesus, often through the work of the Holy Spirit, presents the answer that is unassailable or unrealizable through our humanness.

Jesus also encountered and dealt with evil on a regular basis. The demonic actively pursued Jesus from the time his ministry started until it ended.

(Matthew 4:3-4 ESV) states that after His baptism the Spirit led him into the wilderness to be tempted by the devil. And after He fasted forty days and forty nights he was hungry. The tempter (Devil) came to him and said: "If you are the Son of God, command these stones to become loaves of bread." Jesus countered with "It is written: "Man shall not live by bread alone, but by every word that comes from the mouth of God."

The Devil continues on with two more temptations and promises, which Jesus countered by quoting scripture. The Lord responded by declaring the truth of the written Word. After forty days and nights of fasting the

Devil left and Jesus was met by angels that ministered
to Him.

Experience exposes and erases all the theoretical
platitudes we have learned. 'Pull yourself up by your
bootstraps, or 'get a grip' or 'life goes on.' Many people let
these areas lie silent rather than awaking them by rooting out and exposing hurt, abuse, and damage. A learned
wise man offers evident and obvious insights unlike to a
man living in conjectural theories exhibiting immaturity
and ill choices.

My father likely demonstrated his love the best considering being raised in the 1930's an era of intense work
loads. A twin in a family of eight children where there was
indifference to demonstrative love. He and his brother
spoke a language unbeknown to the rest of the family.
Separation and living apart for a year before being en-
rolled in school appeared to be the only solution to this
problem. It seemed, from accounts, to have changed
the two boys and their personalities. My Dad pined for
his twin brother even in late adulthood and visa-versa.
Emotional damage had occurred never to be altered. His
life demonstrated pain, rejection, and past childhood

loneliness until his death. He was a candidate for emotional/heart healing.

"Numerous research projects in the area of child development have made that conclusion: Babies who are held, hugged and kissed develop a healthier emotional life than those who are left for long periods of time without physical contact."[36]

Further he states "Wise parents, in any culture, are touching parents."[37]

The amazing work of Holy Spirit shines His light on what has been hidden and often buried profoundly deeply. We think we are doing well until the finger of Holy Spirit is placed on a festering boil that is about to burst. A boil that is so irritated and swollen that a little poke causes an eruption. Emotional pain and ills deep within our souls react in the same manner. The eruption can be unexpected, unreasonable and unexplainable. The abundant life that has been planned and promised seems illusive. Some of these heart aches are unable to heal until we experience His touch. These festering boils need to be lanced to allow the vile substance to escape and healing can begin. A sick heart requires the same healing touch.

Dr. Wilfred Kent states "He loved us when we were unlovable. It is something I give without any expectation of anything in return."

Meeting the heart of Jesus changes us from within, which is then demonstrated in our actions. We often come to the crossroad where this divine impacts us with signs. It is at these crossroads undeniable visible and

---

[36] Gary Chapman, The Five Love Languages, (Zondervan Publishing House, 1992) p.115
[37] Gary Chapman, The Five Love Languages, (Zondervan Publishing House, 1992) p.115

invisible, that decisions are made, that lives are changed and will never to be the same again.

"I know of only two alternatives to hypocrisy: perfection or honesty."[38]

Most people would consider their lives satisfactory in how they were raised or where they are now in rearing and background experiences. Regardless of how perfect or imperfect we would consider our upbringing the fact remains we did not have a perfect life nor did we have perfect parents or parenting. There is damage done knowingly or unknowingly. As the Psalmist states in (Psalm 139:23-24 NIV) "Search me, Oh God, and know my heart; try me and know my anxious thoughts. See if there is any offensive way in me, and lead me in the way everlasting."

The Lord does not disappoint in bringing about wholeness into all areas of soul disharmony, but yielding to His scrutiny is the most difficult place of surrender in obedience. Most believers want total honesty and wholeness before the Lord but the question is always in the forefront of our minds: what is the cost? What will I have to face and admit before the Lord before healing and restoration can take place? The price is heart/spirit pain that is uncomfortable in facing the truth, disgrace in hurting His name, non-forgiveness that has leached life, and perhaps wounding those close to us. We can lie to ourselves but vulnerability before Him is an absolute. His light exposes all unseen dark issues. Imagine yourself person standing before the Lord, from this point forward there is no exit or escape from the truth because He is the Spirit of Truth.

---

[38] Philip Yancey, What's So Amazing About Grace, (Zondervan Publishing House, grand Rapids, Michigan 49530, 1997) p.185

So Jesus said to the Jews who had believed in him, "If you abide in my word, you are truly my disciples, and you will know the truth, and the truth will set you free." (John 8: 31, 32 ESV)

Present modern counseling leans toward self help, enlightenment of spirit and obstinate willfulness. This concept misses the requirement in needing a Savior. Truth is the necessary element to move forward. Scripture states in (Jeremiah 17:9-10 ONM) "The heart is deceitful above all things, desperately sick. Who can know it? I, the Lord, search the heart, I try the heart, even to give to each man according to his ways, according to the fruit of his doings."

After our heart is in compliance with truth, movement through the next stages of development and maturity with a new awareness of Him becomes more peaceful.

"We cannot change everything about ourselves simply by trying harder or by will power. If we could, we would not have needed God's grace in the first place."[39]

Taking steps to move forward in the truth allow Holy Spirit to initiate the future undertakings. As we realize how many areas are hidden from our knowledge, we welcome His touch to expose all concealed damage. A person should examine themselves as described in (1 Corinthians 11:31-32) Only by acknowledging that a problem exists can it be repaired in His presence.

Positional points may be reached in each life that require an examination by Holy Spirit. Allowing these significant life changing events to become deep-rooted is one choice, but often not the wisest. The better choice is to seek healing that will require the searchlight be placed

---

[39] Dr. John Townsend, Loving People, (Thomas Nelson, Nashville Tennessee, 2007) p.118

upon and into our hearts. Four words uttered 'Jesus, please help me' will change lives forever.

Wholeness is what we all strive to achieve in our personal walk with Jesus. Only He knows the timing and stages that necessitate wholeness in our lives. Encounters with the living Jesus will mark the mind and soul, often to a depth beyond explanation. The touch of the Father with such power and love defies explanation. These encounters beg the question as to why we do not die instantly. The touch so gentle and measured from the Creator of all knowledge and given by grace through purest love. Such precise and accurate contact makes one stand in awe looking at the designer of heaven and earth.

Chapter 10

Does Love Judge?

D
r. Wayne Dyer states about love in action. "You are not in a state of love whenever you judge another human being. You do not define them with your judgment. You do not define them you define yourself as someone who needs to judge."

There are some in the Church now trying but failing to emulate the absolute love demonstrated by the Lord, causing many in society to wonder which religion is authentic. Church leadership in all categories is expected to hold a position above reproof. Failures stemming from fallen human nature ripple across all denominations, cultures and races. People looking in from outside the church have little understanding of what is meant by grace, and are quick to judge these failures. Believers who have accepted Jesus and His sacrificial death know grace as unmerited favor. Sadly some of this judgment is still justified, though the reproof itself can sometimes be restorative.

We are not here discussing the earthly system of judgment, which has a God-given obligation and responsibility to administer justice. Those holding the office of magistrate, judge, arbitrator or evaluator are placed there for the specific purpose of upholding the law.

We all, however, have a personal sense of justice. Therefore if we believe the Lord is a harsh judge and harsh ruler, we will see life through those filters. If we believe God to be a strong disciplinarian then that is what we will expect Him to be to us. He will hold us to a judgment of intense accountability. He will be unyielding in His control and direction. We will not see His love and grace behind all the difficult and arduous circumstances in our lives.

"External reality, which always reflects back to you your inner state, is then experienced as hostile."[40]

In church cultures there are many judgments placed on believers from what clothes are worn, what foods are eaten, what music may offend, and what language is deemed inappropriate. All of these judgments begin as justifiable guidelines and boundaries existing for the good of all. Regrettably and all too often they evolve into religious systems that bring benefit to no one.

How do these common day-to-day routines influence the way others judge or view our walk with the Lord?

"There is only one real law—the law of the universe." said Dorothy Sayers. "It may be fulfilled either by way of judgment or by the way of grace, but it *must* be fulfilled one way or the other."[41]

Our conscious mind inflicts quick assessments on people who do not hold to our religious standards of beliefs. Within each soul there is immediate approval or

---

[40] Eckhart Tolle, A New Earth (Penguin Group, 375 Hudson Street, New York, 2005) p.203

[41] Philip Yancey, What's So Amazing About Grace? (Zondervan Publishing House, grand Rapids, Michigan 49530, 1997) p.59

disapproval occurring at a rapid pace. The likelihood of condemnations being hurled toward us as people of faith is extremely high considering all humanity is fallible. Within the church body, we continue making, undeserving judgments and rejecting fellow members. As people of faith we must constantly guard and examine our thoughts. First and foremost in guarding our hearts each comment from church members requires a serious examination. People often try to draw us into their battles weighing the right and wrong of their battles. We should guard our hearts therefore avoiding specific volatile positions. Those around us who are not members of the body constantly listen and watch the standards we enact.

"The best way to change other people's behavior is to start changing your own, that is love." (Dr. Daniel Amen)

In the practicality of daily living wrongful words are often spoken and harmful actions taken. Many dreadful happenings are played out daily in the areas of religion. Regrettably many people of faith are involved in these grievous acts.

"Graceless religion tells us we must follow the letter of the rules, and failure will bring eternal rejection."[42]

There is a stench of sulfur in the element of judgment that believers propound to determine and extol the eternal resting place of a soul. The enemy of our soul is constantly trying to entrap us and steer us off course by persuading us to put ourselves in the place of God.

We personally know of a young believer who was so troubled by judgment and guilt that he became convinced he had sinned the unforgivable sin, and that redemption was no longer possible. His inner torment and

---

[42] Philip Yancey, What's So Amazing About Grace? (Zondervan Publishing House, grand Rapids, Michigan 49530, 1997) p.32

mental instability became so severe that after several years of striving, he took his own life. It was the judgment of a religious system that brought such upheaval, anxiety and confusion to the point where balancing all factors became impossible for him. This is an extreme case to be sure, but others in the body of Christ are also sadly suffering, though perhaps not as deeply or obviously as in this case.

(John 12:46-50 ESV) "I have come into the world as light, so that whoever believes in me may not remain in darkness. If anyone hears my words and does not keep them, I do not judge him; for I did not come to judge the world but to save the world. The one who rejects me and does not receive my words has a judge; the word that I have spoken will judge him on the last day. For I have not spoken on my own authority, but the Father who sent me has himself given me a commandment-what to say and what to speak. And I know that his commandment is eternal life. What I say, therefore, I say as the Father has told me."

Jesus, in his first coming, proved Divine love for the world by dying on a cross. To those who believe in Him grace and mercy are offered. The one thief on the cross recognized he was receiving what he was worthy of. Jesus received this thief's declaration of sin and by His mercy and grace said to him "this very day you will be with Me in Paradise." (Luke 23:42-43)

The more we can step out of the picture of our lives and allow Jesus free reign, the more we will experience His power operating in and through our lives. If we could once loosen our grip and let go of the steering wheel, we would gain immeasurable freedom to live in His will. He desires to show us His power but unless we step back, He cannot do what He has conceived for us to do, and that is to lead us in all our ways.

The old adage states that, "all the good in the world are either illegal, immoral or fattening." Here is a quote stating the opposite.

"The Christian ethic that convinces man that he is not on earth to know joy and satisfaction but rather to work and suffer his way to eternal peace with God, is another illustration."[43]

There will be stages in our lives when we are convinced that we are right with the Lord, only to be confronted by Holy Spirit who indicates the contrary. The mystery is there are times when, words of confession are enough, but at other times, the touch of Holy Spirit must go deeper. Events long thought to have been forgiven and forgotten are now brought back in memory. This is where His divine love and knowledge of our soul intercepts the erroneous conclusions of our evaluations. His love exposes and discloses areas of our soul that we are unaware of. It is only here that completion is final and eradication complete.

(Isaiah 9: 6 ESV) "For to us a child is born, to us a son is given; and the *government shall be upon his shoulder*, and his name shall be called Wonderful Counselor, Mighty God, Everlasting Father, Prince of Peace."

Our function is to let God be God.

---

[43] Leo Buscaglia, Love (Ballantine Books, 1972) p.113

Chapter 11

Those That He Loves

One question frequently asked by both believers and non-believers is why God allows earthquakes, sickness, murder or other terrible things to happen to good people? This is a difficult question to which those with theological training offer contrary explanations. Apart from the free will given to humanity the explanations of hermeneutics and eschatology offer little insight.

Earthquakes and tsunamies are becoming a regular occurrences with catastrophic consequences to human life and anything in their paths. On the natural plain it appears that elements of His creation are destroying the very people He created. The forces of nature have been set in motion, and their consequences are at times disastrous to our life and lifestyles. Sickness and suffering continue. New and deadly viruses evolve. Two thousand years ago, forces of nature were set on a course. The earth is now in a tumultuous transition with cataclysmic events occurring everywhere. (Matthew 24:7)

On the human plane, too many people seem out of control taking the lives of their loved ones or engaging in random acts of aggression. These acts are inexplicable to many people, and to the believer they are heinous. (Jeremiah 17: 9 ESV) "The heart is deceitful above all things, and desperately sick; who can understand it?

The only sure position is that of knowing God and the unfathomable depth of His love freely given. His love never fails; it is eternal.

Often when people witness catastrophic events, they directly equate them to an uncaring God who lacks concern or compassion. Their lack of understanding and spiritual knowledge about who God is and how He functions leads them to resistance and judgment. Many of these people do not recognize the sinful condition of the human heart in its unsaved state. They also do not understand that there is an enemy called Satan working against the Lord, His children and all the people of this earth. Satan is operating with great force, tormenting and seeking to kill and destroy.

In the words of Helmut Thielicke, "...the devil succeeds in laying his cuckoo eggs in a pious nest....The sulfurous stench of hell is as nothing compared with the evil odor emitted by divine grace gone putrid."[44]

As we, people of faith, walk through life, we realize that the Lord has a purpose and plan for everyone and for everything that transpires in our lives. Some of these events are difficult to accept and bear, though often their consequences are of our own making. However it is still difficult to come to terms with our decisions, even when in hindsight we can see they are the outcomes to wrongs that we have initiated. In the same way we can also play the blame game for a long time till we realize we have

---

[44] Philip Yancey, What's So Amazing About Grace? (Zondervan Publishing House, grand Rapids, Michigan 49530, 1997) p.31

four fingers pointing back at us when we extend one forward. It can be truly humbling when the Spirit of Truth enlightens us with disclosures of our wrong doing.

Jesus warned us that in this world we would have tribulation but to take heart because He has overcome the world. (John 16: 33 ESV) Some of the stressful circumstances, hardships and suffering that befall us are brought upon us through no fault our own. "Everything is in the process of change including you."[45] Believers are the children of God - a deep spiritual relationship that does not parallel any other relationships we have. The circumstances of life often cause us disorientation in our walk of faith. We need to be reoriented back to Jesus, just like Peter who, after all the discussion, was simply told "Follow me." (John 21:19 ESV)

This walk with Jesus is a love affair that will take us through many discoveries on this journey through life. It is in daily life, through the easy times and the hard times that we come to know Jesus.

"Freedom and discipline are indeed handmaidens; without the discipline of genuine love, freedom is invariably non-loving and destructive."[46]

The trials we face can appear unfair, unjust and unkind. The most difficult task of these times is getting through to God. As we attempt to approach Jesus, it seems as though He has left his throne. Because we are in turmoil, confusion resigns. Our focus shifts to our own emotional state, rather than keeping our eyes on Him. We can take hold of the peace that is waiting there for us, but

---

[45] Leo Buscaglia, Ph. D., Living, Loving & Learning (Ballantine Books, New York, 1982) p.52

[46] M. Scott Peck, M.D., The Road Less Traveled (Simon & Schuster Inc.,1230 Ave., New York, New York, 10020) p.159

the distance is wide from where we are to the lifeline. We need to learn that it is only through His peace that we can bring some semblance of sanity back into our lives.

As we mature in our knowledge of Him, we remind ourselves of past experiences where His love never, ever failed us. Hindsight reminds us of the answers He brought into our minds and the changes He made within our hearts.

"What is essential is invisible to the eye..."[47]

This walk of faith is indeed just that, 'a walk of faith.' We are not given a road map to notify us of all the construction that we are going to face in our journey and how it will affect our personal lives. There are going to be washouts, deep bumps, slippery roads and dead ends! The journey will not have a GPS system that we can use as a guide minute by minute. Some of it is driving blind folded and mistakes not realized until after a full frontal impact. It is most likely now that the Lord has our full attention as He watches his children come to the end of their own power and control. Such crisis should usher us immediately into His presence to seek His help, but often we have a horizontal view rather than a vertical one.

"We see God as a hard taskmaster whose love for us is based on our performance."[48]

We need to recognize that the discipline delivered by the Lord is as varied as the number of personalities in the world. It is suited to the individual like a hand in glove fit. There is no one size fits all in the way He administers his discipline. He has an endless numbers of practical

---

[47] Leo Buscaglia, Ph. D., Living, Loving & Learning (Ballantine Books, New York, 1982) p.91
[48] Heidi Baker, Compelled by Love (Charisma House, 600 Rinehart Road, Lake Mary, Florida 32746) p.100

applications specifically made for each person and their condition. These are custom made for the person involved because He knows our thoughts and heart. This love is designed to meet us where we need the most assistance or rectification.

The Lord's discipline never involves fear. (1 John 4:18 NIV) tells us, "There is no fear in love. But perfect love drives out fear, because fear has to do with punishment. The one who fears is not made perfect in love."

The Lord's discipline to His children always involves seeing His children through eyes of love. It is never vindictive. His loves covers and forgives even though we may have discredited and humiliated ourselves. His discipline is always firm yet flavored with the most heart soothing love, like a salve being applied.

Contrary to His treatment of His children, He called out the Pharisees and religious leaders of His day, embarrassing and shaming them, and systematically confronting their religion-based public antics. (Matthew 6:2)

But for His children, "As the heart is purified, we can see Him with greater and greater clarity. I want to be fully possessed by His Holy Spirit until I am completely overshadowed by God. I want to be utterly overtaken."[49]

The Lord is good in all that He does and His ways are perfect. We are the people that He loves and disciplines in love.

"Those whom I love, I reprove and discipline, so be zealous and repent." (Revelation 3:19 ESV)

---

[49] Heidi Baker, Compelled by Love (Charisma House, 600 Rinehart Road, Lake Mary, Florida 32746) p.90

Chapter 12

Love: The Last Word

All the words on love - stories, revelations, descriptions and insights, will never give credence to the infinite realm available to us.

There is no height, depth or width that can ever plumb 'love's' borders. Love has been described in many languages, and cultures, but will it ever be completely known? It is impossible to find spoken language that can faithfully explore its significance or value. Beyond this earthly experience, there is the love that is the promise of God's eternal plan for the redeemed.

Love has the ability to be tangible to our senses but never fully grasped or explained in our intellect. It is always elusive, equivocal and evasive, but it is clearly substantial.

"Pierre Teilhard de Chardin put it this way: "The conclusion is always the same: Love is the most powerful and still the most unknown energy of the world."[50]

---

[50] Dr. Wayne W. Dyer, The Power of Intention (Hay House, Inc. P.O. Box 5100, Carlsbad, CA 92018-5100, 2004) p.27

Love can have multiple avenues of expression though no single explanation can fully seize hold of its expansive significance.

For us to put love in context, our minds would expand to dimensions able to encompass the size of the world, outer space and all galaxies. Grasping the infinite knowledge or understanding of this unconditional love is only a tiny morsel in our human intelligence.

God expressed His part by sending His son Jesus. "The son of man came to seek and save the lost" (Luke 19:10 ESV)

What other way would God use to prove His love?

To us, the love Jesus has for this world is unfamiliar, largely unknown and overwhelming. How can it be that an act of death would suffice to bring forth love and new life? That is the greatest gift given to man. The pathway of redemption was met by Jesus for us to enter salvation without limits or bounds. It is only through the self-centered wisdom of man where limitations rule.

"Immature love says: "I love you because I need you." Mature love says: "I need you because I love you." Gandhi

A song recorded by the Gaither vocal Group has a thought provoking lyric "If coal can turn to diamonds, if sand can turn to pearls, if a worm can turn into a butterfly than love can turn the world."

Love is like an ever-revolving door. We allow some people into our personal space and lives, but others we hold at arm's length. Love will take our individual personal relationships only where we choose. How many offenses can we overlook and forgive? When we affirm and forgive all others, the boundaries of our love expand.

The Lord loves unconditionally regardless of obstinate behavior, wrong beliefs, and sinful activity past or present. His love remains unconditional regardless of our imperfections or flaws.

His love is demonstrated to all people and there is nothing more that He can do in proving unconditional love.

Does His love depend on how many times a confession is made or how many times we repent? Does it depend on how much you donate financially to the church or charitable organizations? How about the way you treat you mother, spouse, neighbor or child? Wrongful events that cause harm and damage are always in need of correction, but His love can reach into the most despicable of our actions and errors in life to console, forgive and restore. As His children there is nothing that can separate us from His heavenly love.

It is not conditionally based on the work we do or don't do. Love met the condition of sin through Jesus dying on the cross. There is nothing to add or subtract, all accounts have been paid in full.

Love can and does manifest itself in many and various circumstances in one's life. It is re-defining our lives constantly through new growth, maturity and deepening love. The progression develops and expands our hearts to look only to Him the all sufficient one.

Those most defiant against Jesus are often some of the most lonely and needy. Anger can turn inward and can become self-destructive. Self-pity may turn into resentment and bitterness. Obstinate behavior demonstrates a hardness of heart that places blame on others. These are just some examples of unpleasant characteristics that can be placed at the feet of Jesus and He has the power to bring peace and harmony.

The more a person recognizes the amount of love Jesus has available to give, the more that person will receive and be able to pass it on. The battle to allow more love into our lives proceeds from within our hearts. It is a battle against selfishness and residues of hardness.

"I only love God as much as I love the person I love the least."[51]

Christ presented symbols of His impending sacrifice. As we look at love and what love offered us through His death the symbols become even more significant. This becomes a once-and-for-all fulfillment of the last word spoken allowing entry into the new covenant life. "And he took bread, and when he had given thanks, he broke it and gave it to them, saying, "This is my body, which is given for you. Do this in remembrance of me." (Luke 22:19 ESV)

Mother Teresa once said: "When Jesus came into the world, He loved it so much that He gave His life for it. He wanted to satisfy our hunger for God. And what did He do? He made Himself the Bread of Life. He became small, fragile, and defenseless for us. Bits of bread can be so small that even a baby can chew it. He became the Bread of Life to satisfy our hunger for God, our hunger for love."[52]

Love's last word is remembering that in Jesus the price has been paid in full. Compensation for entry has been met. The next step falls into the court of each individual who has the choice through faith to accept or deny His existence and Lordship.

Those who find Him will never be disappointed in His perpetual love.

---

[51] Philip Yancey, What's So Amazing About Love (Zondervan Publishing House, grand Rapids, Michigan 49530, 1997) p.144

[52] Heidi Baker, Compelled by Love (Charisma House, 600 Rinehart Road, Lake Mary, Florida 32746) p.67-68

Chapter 13

Love at Its Depth

When we examine the many avenues of love, the foundational truth is that Jesus showed the depth of his love by taking the bitter cup of sin even unto death. He himself was clean and perfect. Therefore, taking on the sin of the world hardly seems just or fair. In His last remaining hours on earth, He asked His Father if this cup could be removed. (Matthew 26:39 ESV) Shortly after that, He also asked his disciples to pray... "that you may not enter into temptation. The Spirit is indeed willing but the flesh is weak" (v. 41)

The demonic actively confronted Him. The Pharisees and religious rulers questioned Him. Everywhere, He encountered and dealt with tests of His perfect nature and righteous love on a regular basis.

Matthew tells us that after His baptism the devil took him to the holy city and had Him stand on the highest point of the temple. "If you are the Son of God" he said, "throw yourself down."

Jesus countered, "It is also written: Do not put the Lord your God to the test." Then the devil took him to a very high mountain and showed him all the kingdoms of the world and their splendor. "All of this I will give you," he said, "If you will bow down and worship me."

Jesus said to him, "Away from me Satan. For it is written: Worship the Lord your God, and serve him only." (Matthew 4:7-10 NIV)

His servant heart is benevolent towards the people He created. The numerous ways that He attends to us are as varied as the galaxies in His creation. Some ways are very evident, others are more subtle. Some are concealed but others are easy to recognize. Changes that have taken place in the inner core or heart of individuals are made evident by their outward behavior. Their countenances often transmit a buoyant, carefree attitudes. They are hopeful and positive. There is a 'light' they transmit that speaks of joy, peace and rest.

On the other hand, body language can speak volumes when people are angry or upset. Often, I have been in association with a person who suddenly demonstrate an outburst of displeasure over a meal that is served, or have a strong, aggressive outburst complete with harsh tone about some topic under discussion. These reactions appear totally inappropriate to the events in question.

"Man learns evil in the same manner in which he learns good. If he believes in a world of evil he will respond suspiciously, fearfully and be constantly searching for and assuredly find the evil he seeks."[53]

Jesus confronted and conquered all temptations and obstacles before Him. This is also where all of our battles are won or lost, at the inner core of our being, where we make the long-lasting decisions that effect our lives. It is here that true change must take place. The mind and the

---

[53] Leo Buscaglia, Love (Ballantine Books, 1972) p.125

heart, or soul, are always in conflict. The mind forever desires to lead the body. Training it to follow the Holy Spirit is a difficult venture. Only through grace given by the Lord and heart felt devotion from us will the Holy Spirit lead the body.

The inner-life's spirit requires constant alteration if it is to hear Holy Spirit's voice. Deep in the recesses of the soul, we all have wounds and gaping rips that begin at the start of life and continue to our present age.

The term 'inner healing' has been around and practiced for a considerable length of time. Pastor John Wimber pioneered a movement that led to swift awareness of issues, repair and blessing in what Holy Spirit desired to modify in the heart. Many thousands if not hundreds of thousands embraced this extraordinary transformation in their lives. Two more pioneers were John and Paula Sanford who wrote many books in conjunction with hosting schools where deep painful memories and experiences were wiped clean.

Inner healing is one of those events when the divine draws you into a realm that many have experienced though few can explain. As this author said, "At once I had the strange sensation as if a dimmer switch had turned the inside of my entire body to maximum power."[54]

This power of Jesus is so incredible, undeniable and yet inexplicable in understanding verbiage. These divine touches are miracles of healing, life changing experiences that are verified by changed lives.

'Inner healing' or 'emotional healing' is always indicative of the deep changes that are not visible with the

---

[54] Eckhart Tolle....A New Earth (Penguin Group, 375 Hudson Street, New York, 2005) p.175

naked eye. These damaged crevices in our hearts require the light of truth that only Holy Spirit can illuminate and heal by His power, divine appointment and love.

This heart-pain demands attention and care. Our emotions require the healing balm of the Spirit. First we must choose to allow Him free access. Then agreeing the Holy Spirit is the Spirit of Truth, choose to follow the course laid out by Him. He will present the area we are to clearly identify from a number of options such as forgiveness, repentance, a touch of divine love, or perhaps the rooting out bitterness or anger. There are numerous practical and necessary interventions. Wholeness, likened to a release, then places us in a brand-new relationship with Jesus. The abundant life that has been planned and promised begins anew. This renewing has been decreed for our highest good. It is no longer illusive like some dream of possibilities. As we surrender and grow in the Spirit, this healing becomes a regular occurrence.

Sometimes our spiritual awareness is limited by what we have been taught but not experienced. Actual experience confirms that all the theoretical platitudes we have heard or studied may be in error to some degree. How obviously better are the actions and insights of a Godly wise man than those of a man living in manic emotionalism exhibiting immaturity and ill choices. "A fool gives full vent to his spirit, but a wise man quietly holds it back." (Proverbs 29:11 ESV)

Meeting the heart of Jesus changes us from within, which then finds expression in our actions. We often come to a crossroads where the divine impacts us with undeniable power. It is at these crossroads that our lives are changed never to be the same again.

A young man whom I have known for many years experienced both physical and emotional abuse at the hand his father, and as a consequence, he struggled with bouts of depression for most of his adult life. His downward emotional turns were always focused on that abusive relationship magnifying its inherent lack of respect together with his inability to defend himself. Whenever these haunting thoughts of memory surfaced, foremost present was appeared his inability to forgive. Forgiveness here was the key that would unlock the door to his torment. To this day, this man is a disciple of Jesus, but one who is unable to let go of this past event even though his Dad has been deceased for many years. If he was to choose to enact forgiveness and allow Jesus to absorb this burden, it would bring peace and tranquility. The account would be settled although not completely forgotten.

Encounters by the living Father leave a mark on the mind and soul often to a depth incomprehensible to explain but the touch of Jesus defies explanation. One might expect that direct contact with divine power would be fatal to us. In reality, the power is administered perfectly, His touch so gentle and measured, that one stands in awe of its precision and accuracy.

"I had a theoretical biblical knowledge regarding healing and the revelatory ministry of the Holy Spirit, but Wimber had a practical knowledge and experience in how these things actually work."[55]

Proven true time and again is the fact He does not disappoint in bringing about wholeness into all areas of our being, though yielding to this scrutiny is one of the hardest places to arrive at in our walk with the Lord. Do

---

[55] Jack Deere, Surprised By The Power Of The Spirit (Zondervan Publishing House, Grand Rapids, Michigan, 1993) p.37

we desire to be totally genuine and vulnerable before the Lord? This question is always in the forefront: what is the cost? What will I have to transverse and deal with before healing can take place? Not only will I have to be totally honest but also totally vulnerable about all of my inner-life's issues past and present. It is as if the Lord's eyes become transfixed on our issues and the response is in our court. There is no escaping or running away from truth because He is the truth.

We want to be standing in truth regardless of how uncomfortable or painful it might be. After our heart is in compliance with truth there is a godlike shift that moves from insensitive thinking into a spirit that is malleable and pliable.

As the medieval German mystic Mesiter Eckhart wrote: "The bodily food we take is changed into us, but the spiritual food we receive changes us into itself; therefore divine love is not taken into us, for that would make two things. But divine love takes us into itself, and we are one with it."[56]

What is required is to answer *yes* to the promptings by Holy Spirit. We need to realize that our truth may not line up with the Lord's, truth and that it is imperative to experience His truth. (Psalm 51: 6 ESV) states "Behold, you delight in truth in the inward being, and you teach me wisdom in the secret heart."

We all strive to achieve wholeness in our personal walk with Jesus. Only He knows the timing and stages that underpin these encounters. To understand love at its depth necessitates our co-operation in being totally candid, available, and willing to allow Him to write

---

[56] Bernie S. Siegel, M.D., Love, Medicine & Miracles (Harper & Row, 10 East 53rd Street, New York, N.Y. 10022, 1986) p.182

the story of our lives. Yes, being vulnerable and broken can be painful but the reward is freedom from weighty encumbrances.

In the Garden of Eden, Adam and Eve felt shame before God when they realized they were naked, but only after they had eaten the forbidden fruit. Previous to this they walked in the garden with Him naked and unashamed. (Genesis 3:8-10 ESV)

Standing before Him defenseless and totally exposed brings us back to love at its depth. It returns us to the state of Adam and Eve before the fall. There is no shame or guilt. This is love at its depth.

Chapter 14

Miracles and Healing

S ometimes the stated purpose for healing is to bring glory to God. That was one of the primary purposes in raising Lazarus from the dead. Jesus told the disciples, "This sickness will not end in death. No it is for God's glory so that God's Son may be glorified through it" John 11: 4 And then he said to Martha, "Did I not tell you that if you believed, you would see the glory of God?" (John 11:40 ESV)

Jesus also healed to establish that He was the resurrection and the life.

In counseling or any type of ministry the greatest gift is to see the Lord Jesus touch, restore and heal. At times miracles take place and the healing is immediate, while healing at other times it is a gradual improvement over time. Both types of healing are miraculous, both are divine interventions.

A very common question in all circles of ministry or in daily life is why are not all the sick healed? We step forward with a strong conviction and desire to see the miraculous. Often, we are blessed but at other times, our requests are not met. Disappointment and disillusionment can follow as we question why was that person was not healed?

Even so to witness the power of Jesus healing a paralyzed arm or, to see a young crippled girl walking, growths disappearing from a young woman's face or demonic oppression and possession released is infinitely more satisfying than the disappointments. There is no greater kingdom blessing this side of heaven.

As it says in the Course of Miracles, "Miracles are merely the sign of your willingness to follow the Holy Spirit's plan."[57]

We see in (Luke 17:17-18 NIV) that after healing ten lepers only one would return, falling on his face, thanking and glorifying God. There was a sense of disappointment when Jesus asked, "then where are the other nine? Was no one found to return and give praise to God except this foreigner?" Then He said to him "Rise and go your faith has made you well." We are to continue along the path of prayer and asking regardless of previous experiences.

Healing and miracles are another demonstration of His extraordinary love for us, and His compassion and empathy are vibrant and alive today. Great healing ministries are emerging with documented reversals in a variety of conditions and illnesses. Healing did not end after Jesus Christ's resurrection. In fact the likelihood is that they will increase as the end of the age unfolds.

Stepping out in faith to pray for the sick is another choice we are given. The act of healing is not our responsibility, ours is but to ask for the Father's power to be demonstrated. His touch is evident to the person receiving it as is the miraculous result. Fear is the only

---

[57] Dr. Wayne Dyer, Your Sacred Self (HarperCollins, 10 East 53rd Street, New York, NY, 2003) p.79

element that will keep us bound and keep us from risking
to pray for someone's healing. We are required by faith
to take that first step forward. If we are not part of this
divine plan as His children to pray for healing who will go
in Jesus name?

We have been given the responsibility and privilege of
taking Christ out into the world. As His children it is in-
cumbent upon us to "Go into all the world and proclaim
the gospel....they will lay their hands on the sick, and they
will recover." (Mark 16:15-18 ESV)

The cost to us could be embarrassment but the gain is
for the glory of Christ. He is the all sufficient one through
life and in death.

Chapter 15

There is No Fear in Love

One of the most amazing and astonishing verses in the NIV Bible boldly states: "There is no fear in love, but perfect love drives out fear, because fear has to do with punishment. The one who fears is not made perfect in love." (1 John 4:18 ESV)

Look at this verse's first phrase. How many times have we found that to be true in life?

Many of us have been bruised, walked on, lied to and discarded in the pursuit of infamous love, or in those relationships where we thought love would prevail. These words have a ring to them that could have been written for a country and western heartbreak cowboy song. Unfortunately it is not just a song but reality in life. Our minds and emotions race through these situations, becoming increasingly confused and full of turmoil.

"Those who measure such things estimate that our minds have sixty thousand thoughts during the waking hours of every day. Sixty thousand times each day something called a new thought enters our consciousness and then exits, while another thought enters."[58]

That is an astounding number of thoughts per day, considering that every action that we take begins first and foremost in our brains and its thoughts, some negative and some positive. Unless the brain can be taught to listen to the heart, wherever the brain leads, the body follows.

"The brain is ill-equipped to translate the subtle nature and spiritual magnitude of love energy events."[59]

If there are anxious thoughts, they can trigger the desire to perform any number of activities. Emotional reactions could include anger, confusion, distress, or fear, though exactly how these responses surface remain with the individual. Awareness of where these thoughts can lead should always be of great concern. Examining our thoughts constantly would be one of the solutions to negativity and irrational ideas. These irrational ideas can lead us down unprofitable paths counter to our best interests.

The likelihood of being harmed in any loving relationships is equally as great as falling and scraping a knee in childhood. It is going to happen repeatedly. We are the walking wounded when it comes to love. Mere mention of the word will often stir up some emotion. Flashbacks of past situations, comments or actions can bring up old wounds within the soul.

Because the full development of the brain is not until after the age of twenty-five or later, with the cognitive

---

[58] Paul Pearsall, Ph. D., The Heart's Code, The Heart's Code (Broadway Books,New York, NY 1999) p.26
[59] Paul Pearsall, PhD, The Heart's Code, The Heart's Code, (Broadway Books,New York, NY 1999) p.176

area developing last, our associations as we develop are almost guaranteed to be impaired. These associations can be carried into adulthood and perhaps will never be challenged. It is a sad fact of life that the mental coding system of previous experiences must be dismantled for these adults to have a true understanding of His love.

People see their human relationships much like they see their relationship to God. They do not see God as kind, compassionate, loving, empathetic, and only wanting their good.

There is a process involved in ridding ourselves of the unpleasant memories about earlier events in our lives. We have access to this healing, which sometimes we need on a daily basis, though we are slow to enact His help.

If we continue to struggle in our personal relationships, this may influence our interactions with Jesus. The inference from (1 John 4:18 ESV) is that the one who fears is not made perfect in love, is that we are miles away from knowing eternal love, and that our earthly associations may impair our awareness of, or severely compromise divine love.

Love carries the responsibility to accept and trust completely in a relationship regardless of the circumstances. More than just trusting in our own feelings, we also believe in the other's loyalty. Fear should have no place in any relationship especially where love is declared. Succumbing to fright, dread or alarm is an unwelcome option because our heart will suffer discourse and upheaval.

In our human relationships areas of panic seem to creep in easily. The unknown is always a threat that may grow each day. Somehow this is always related back to the Lord and whether He knows and cares about our well-being. Can we trust Him in every area including our very lives?

There is an old Irish proverb that says this so well, "Fear knocked at the door, and faith answered, and no one was there."[60]

Fear stems from doubts we have about His promises to us. Can we release control and put our life into His care? The antidote to fear is faith.

The Lord's perfect love drives out fear. If love was influenced by our imperfect performance, then under any legal system, fear would prompt us to expect punishment. The only perfect love without fear known to this world comes from God through Jesus. All other paths are counterfeits. The enemy is a master at counterfeiting. He leads many down the paths of fictitious lies and half-truths.

The second part of (1 John 4:18 NIV) states: "The one who fears is not made perfect in love." What does this say about people who believe they are living in this perfect divine love but are still experiencing fear? This fear negates God's perfect love. So, how do we attain this measure of love in ourselves?

There is a process in knowing Jesus and His perfect love. Through the trials, testing, tribulations and conquering of obstacles we learn to trust in His love for us and see that He proves His love for us daily. Many times this is where the most profound lessons are being learned as fear begins to dissipate and a knowing love replaces fear. As His love is proved to us we begin to trust Him by learning to stand on His word. It is His faithfulness over time that shows us our love can be without fear.

---

[60] Dr. Wayne W. Dyer, There's A Spiritual Solution to Every Problem (HarperCollins, 10 East 53rd Street, New York, NY, 2003) p.202

Not many among us could say we don't fear for our financial futures today with the shaking of the world economies or the real presence of catastrophes like earthquakes, nuclear fallout, wild fires, hurricanes and tornadoes. How do we arrive at the point where it can be said I have no fear because I am certain of the Lord's love?

In (Hebrews 12:2) we see that Jesus is the founder and perfecter of our faith. He allows our circumstances to teach us, even our errors and missteps, to gain more of His wisdom and grace.

A child is totally dependent on the adults in his or her life. Their necessity is for love. Physical, emotional, and spiritual care is essential for development. The same prerequisite applies to believers; to be child-like waiting on Jesus, asking for help, and trusting Him for all our needs.

Perfected love is like having a child-like faith totally dependent on their parent, except for believers their faith is in Jesus. When love is the foundation, there is security and fear has been driven out. This truth then gradually becomes our anchor and our footing. Thereafter, nurturing and growth will continue based on the willingness of our hearts to continually seek Jesus. This kind of love cannot be duplicated nor can it be explained.

"Beliefs restrict you. Knowings empower you."[61]

When the eyes of our hearts are continually focused on Him for direction and guidance, this eliminates peripheral elements that try to bring fear to the forefront. Security lies in the position of our focus; knowing not to look to the right or to the left.

Being perfected in love gives the ability to state with total resolve that the peace of the Lord belongs to his

---

[61] Dr. Wayne W. Dyer, Your Sacred Self (HarperCollins Publishers, 10 East 53rd. Street, New York, N.Y. 10022) p.100

children whatever their situation. Fear is given neither a place nor a hearing. In consequence, we stand secure in the power of love's ability to block all threatening fear.

We stand with boldness, which is one mark of the Spirit. (2 Timothy 1:7 ESV) "For God gave us a spirit not of fear but of power and love and self-control."

Chapter 16

When Love Hurts

Most of humanity has loved and lost. When hurt by love, we can be exposed to deep, lasting, indescribable pain. What elements are required to heal and move us forward before we can love wholehearted again?

The heart fortunately is very pliable and malleable and able to rebound even though the emotional damage still leaves deep scars and bruises. Unless there is instant forgiveness, the pain lingers on and the need for healing remains.

Jesus prophesied after He and the disciples sung a hymn that his disciples would slip away. Peter, being the outspoken one, declared he would not. Jesus replied that this night, before the rooster crows, Peter would deny him three times. Peter vehemently announced he would not deny Jesus. Not only Peter but all the other disciples agreed with the statement. Their sincerity was genuine, but their actions failed them. This became a promise, to their friend Jesus, they were unable to keep.

It was not only Peter who denied Jesus three times, but all the disciples left him in his time of need. Jesus emphatically states in his prophetic knowing that He would be deserted by the ones who said they loved Him. He was overwhelmed by sorrow and distress as He contemplated death on the cross, but while in prayer three separate times He came back to find the disciples sleeping. In His time of need and emotional suffering He asked Peter "So could you not watch with me one hour?" (Matthew 26:40 ESV) In their earnestness to demonstrate their love and devotion, they had all reinforced Peter's statement declaring their commitment to Him. They all failed and deserted Him. It might seem to us that love failed, and this failure may have caused injury and hurt to Jesus. But from all reports, Jesus never held any offense or waited to receive any apology. There is no indication that this instance of betrayal deterred Him, emotionally upset Him or caused irreconcilable division.

There are many other instances where He also suffered personal injury without reprisal, such as Judas betraying him after years spent in his company.

"To love in the midst of pain, to forgive in the midst of evil, to comfort in the midst of agony, to bring peace in a time of war is the heart of God."[62]

Jesus merely continued his mission and then after his resurrection he appeared to Peter and told him "to feed my lambs, to tend my sheep also to feed my sheep." (John 21:15-17 ESV) He next prophesied the end of Peter's life, how others would lead him around and feed him indicating Peter would be blind. Peter continues to speak to Jesus while looking in John's direction and asks, "What about this man?" Jesus said to him, "If it is my will that he remain until I come, what is that to you? Follow me!"

---

[62] Heidi Baker, Compelled by Love (Charisma House, 600 Rinehart Road, Lake Mary, Florida 32746) p.113

(John 21:22 ESV) Jesus forcefully states to Peter not to wonder about others but focus on his own relationship with Christ by stating emphatically to "follow me."

Jesus never missed a step in fulfilling His purpose in coming to earth. He had good reason to scrub these men from his list of faithful followers but he didn't. His purpose outweighed the minor stumbling blocks placed along His path. He never veered from this purpose and calling. The plan was clear. Christ was to be the fulfillment of the law and the conqueror of death.

One lesson for us to learn from Christ is that forgiveness releases us from being in emotional bondage to the persons who harmed us. We are not held by their power or under their control if we choose to forgive. We likely could fill volumes listing the harm done to us through lies, mistreatment, unkind words, theft, and treason. Legalism allows us to retaliate but under grace and love that is not an option. Our journey involves stages in comprehending mercy, which allows us to offer unsolicited and unmerited forgiveness.

It is commanded that we forgive as we have been forgiven. "...as the Lord has forgiven you, so you also must forgive." (Col 3: 13 ESV)

Here we need to guard against the superficial. Our initial offering of repentance and forgiveness may not speak to the core of the injury. These harmful areas of our character may be entrenched in our mind, body, emotion and will. Later, with deeper awareness in us as Holy Spirit directly touches the root point, a more authentic forgiveness and healing takes place. Because He can see and touch areas hidden to us, we are then brought into a new level of His knowledge and healing. He knows we hide behind our platitudes and efforts often require more specific depth of healing. The mystery of healing is that only He alone can illuminate the depth to the root of the suffering, and it is the light of Holy Spirit that can restore to wholeness.

"In *The Art Of Forgiving* Lewis Smedes makes the striking observation that the Bible portrays God going through progressive stages when he forgives, much as we humans do. First, God rediscovers the humanity of the person who wronged him by removing the barrier created by sin. Second, God surrenders his right to get even, choosing instead to bear the cost in his own body. Finally, God revises his feelings toward us, finding a way to 'justify' us so that when he looks upon us he sees his own adopted children, with his divine image restored."[63]

This world struggles under the heavy schemes of oppression enacted by the enemy and his minions. Offenses usually instill anger and the Lord is clear that we are not to let anger consume us not even for a day so that we do not give opportunity to the devil. (Ephesian 4:27 ESV)

"If you're going to seek revenge, you'd better dig two graves. Practice letting go of injured feelings with love and pardon and the spiritual solutions to most of your problems will be activated. Let go and let God..."[64]

The ones closest to us seem to hurt us the most because the greater we love the more defenseless we are. Offenses that we are unable to forgive leave a vulnerability in our soul that the Enemy can attack. We then give the Enemy the legal right to torment and harass us. For shear self protection, forgiveness is an absolutely

---

[63] Philip Yancey, What's So Amazing About Grace? (Zondervan Publishing House, grand Rapids, Michigan 49530, 1997) p.96
[64] Wayne W. Dyer, There's A Spiritual Solution To Every Problem (Harper Collins,, 10 East 53rd Street, New York, N.Y. 10022, 2001) p.196

essential requirement in dealing with any hurt, wounding or offense against our own person.

Have we arrived at the point where we can say I have been hurt in love but the wounding has not caused me to give up on love? Considering previous life experiences, are the risks in love really worth it?

Questions like these have answers that vary from one person to the next. It is such an individual event that there is not one pat answer. Some of us forgive easily. Some of us hold on to the pain if only because it is easier to go back to past behaviors than adopt new ones. Self-preservation behaviors that have worked in the past often remain our first choice. The most comfortable position is to not rock the boat – to ignore the hurt. Under the Lord's system, however, confronting the uncomfortable within us allows for grace and forgiveness as well as emotional healing.

"Fear holds close, love holds dear. Fear grasps, love lets go. Fear rankles, love soothes. Fear attacks, love amends."[65]

As the Lord's prayer declares He knows what we have need of before we ask. Then He taught them how pray using a few very poignant words. (Matt. 6:9-14 ESV) He speaks about debtors and the need to forgive our debtors, and if we don't forgive them their trespasses neither will ours be forgiven. There is a direct correlation between our forgiving people and whether the Lord will forgive us. It is a very important point to keep the relationship open between the Lord and ourselves. This is to be taken very seriously in our walk with Him. We need to keep short account balance in all our relationships, present and future.

---

[65] Neale Donald Walsch, Conversations with God (Penguin Putnam Inc., 375 Hudson Street, New York, N.Y. 1995) p.19

On the one hand, short accounting will not allow emotional sores to form or negative feelings to grow and multiply. On the other hand, antagonistic attitudes and upsets will lead us further down the path away from peace, love and the Lord. The enemy of our soul is always waiting for an opportunity to escalate the hurt and play havoc with the situation. By opting for the ideal of forgiveness we circumvent the enemies plan. By immediately forgiving, we cut him off at the pass and He now has no further grounds to accuse or attack.

"You have to take the responsibility for choosing and defining your own life."[66]

Our lives are perceptibly enhanced on short accounts with Jesus, therefore repentance and forgiveness define a major part in our responsibility in this relationship.

His love and grace is unending and extravagantly available when love hurts.

---

[66] Leo Buscaglia, Ph. D., Living, Loving & Learning (Ballantine Books, New York, 1982) p.168

Chapter 17

The Ultimate Love

Ascribing the word *'ultimate'* to a description of love suggests the crowning purpose of the life that we were created to experience and express. The expression *'ultimate'* love, does it exist and can it be referenced only to the Lord? Can we mortals display this level of love to people we connect with throughout our lives? Can this *ultimate/* supreme love be accomplished this side of heaven?

Perhaps people like Mother Theresa or others like her, who give selflessly, come to our remembrance. To witness such devotion expressed through caring is an example of inspired self-sacrificing love.

Jesus said in (John 5:39-40 ESV) "You search the Scriptures because you think that in them you have eternal life; and it is they that bear witness about me. Yet you refuse to come to me that you may have life."

Jesus emphatically states searching the scriptures will not bring eternal life. Scriptures nourish, teach and transform us but, more than that, the Scriptures speak of the one who gives life - Jesus. (John 5:39 ESV)

This eternal life is obtained by a personal intimate friendship and a flourishing relationship with the Lord.

"Relationships do not grow or remain stimulating without conscious effort. We must take the time to enrich our lives and therefore our love, or we are merely coexisting. Complacency kills."[67]

Complacency is a place in which we can all find ourselves at one time or another. Being lukewarm appears to irritate the Lord as we see in (Rev. 3:16 ESV) He would rather we not be tepid or indifferent as being lukewarm is repugnant to Him. At times complacency or self-satisfaction becomes a very comfy spot to settle into. This can be a place that captures our heart. Unfortunately this stops our spiritual growth and staying there is not an option. The deep cry of our heart will continually be searching for more of Him, the infinite Christ. If we ignore this plea we will become indifferent and stale. Stale water soon becomes toxic for human consumption. Drinking from streams of *living water* brings life to our soul and spirit. (John 4:10 ESV)

There is an old adage that states "He loves us right where we are but loves us too much to leave us there." (author unknown) Christ's desire is that we continually choose to move forward in His direction.

"You have to take the responsibility for choosing and defining your own life."[68]

Planted within our hearts, is the yearning to experience more of our infinite, measureless Jesus. There is a crying out to Jesus to take us ever deeper in the

---

[67] Leo Buscaglia, Born For Love (Ballantine Books, New York, 1992) p.166

[68] Leo Buscaglia, Ph. D., Living, Loving & Learning (Ballantine Books, New York, 1982) p.168

knowledge of Him, to explore new heights and depths of His character that will take us beyond our known boundaries. As God's children, a purpose and a call has been placed deep within our hearts and we delight ourselves in Him. (Psalm 37: 4 ESV)

"The resurrection shows the limitlessness of God's reliability. 'Strong as death is love' says the (Song of Songs 8:6) but the resurrection proves that God's love is stronger than death. Now we are secure and safe in the love of God. Now we know that there is no limit to it."[69]

Devout Christian believers have sought unconditional love on one level and perhaps infrequently have achieved it on another. To love divinely as God does is perhaps the most unknowingly sought after goal in the entire Christian world. Many seek and extol people who proclaim this kind of love but who then follow the most incomprehensible teachings trying to embrace it. Everyone one who speaks and declares love may not be a credible source. The enemy of our soul is a deceiver, thief and a liar deceiving many.

1 Corinthians 13 is recognized as the love chapter and gives the most superlative description of love ever carried into human language.

(1 Corinthians 13:4-8 NIV) speaks about the high beckoning call of love for each man and woman. This portion of scripture clearly describes sixteen important elements of what love is. "Love is: (1) patient, (2) kind, (3) does not envy, (4) does not boast, (5) is not proud (6) is not rude, (7) is not self-seeking, (8) is not easily angered, (9) keeps no records of wrongs, (10) does not delight in evil, (11) rejoices with the truth, (12) always protects, (13)

---

[69] Peter G. van Breemen, S..J., As Bread That is Broken (Dimension Books, Inc., Denville, New Jersey, 1974) p.169

always trusts, (14) always hopes, (15) always perseveres. (16) Love never fails. The greatest character quality that we can obtain is love.

"True love never forces."[70]

Paul further states spiritual gifts without love are worthless, but that love lasts forever.

The fruit of the Spirit coming forth from love are: joy, peace, patience, kindness, goodness, faithfulness, gentleness, and self control.

Not seeing any such fruit in our own lives points to the problem being on our side of the ledger and not on the Lord's. These may be issues buried deep within our hearts that require resolution. We may have unbelief, hardness of heart, an unforgiving spirit, bitterness, anger or other unsettled issues before Him. Therefore Holy Spirit's work has been stymied.

The Holy Spirit does not bring forth hate, deceit, fear, rebellion, malice, etc. These are all attributed to the work of the enemy. The fruit of the Spirit only attained with *love in the Spirit* or *ultimate love* divinely given. This is divine - Jesus - love operating and overflowing beyond our known potential. Failure to demonstrate a particular fruit of His Spirit is indicative of an area that requires attention.

In (Galatians 5:22 NIV) "But the fruit of the Spirit is love..." Here the word *fruit* in the original language of the text is singular not plural. Any of these fruits produced by the Spirit originates in love. The fruit of the Spirit is then described by the eight traits listed above in (1 Corinthians 13:4-8 ESV) This then is the indisputable or

---

[70] William P. Young,The Shack (Windblown Media, 4680 Calle Norte, Newbury Park,CA, 2007) p 190

supreme love when our actions, words and deeds exhibit one or more of these fruit.

"The law *defined* love; Christ *demonstrated* love."[71]

However, life in the Spirit requires His supernatural work from within. This is not a power that we create or initiate. This power is a gift from God to all believe in His son. Ultimate love, or love of the Spirit, is the only truly authentic, altruistic form of love. Some people operate under sheer willpower and the results can be impressive, but operating by resolve pales in comparison to the genuine expression of love through the Holy Spirit.

(John 6: 63 ESV) "It is the Spirit who gives life; the flesh is no help at all. The words that I have spoken to you are Spirit and life."

Love is initiated in the heart, and is distributed by words spoken and with hands outstretched. Our acts of love intensify as we listen to Holy Spirit and follow in obedience. He will empower us to increase our daily acts of love under His authority.

Ultimate love or love in the Spirit will be recognized by the fruit we bear and reflect the character of God.

---

[71] Josh McDowell and Norm Geisler, Love is Always Right (Word Publishing, Dallas Texas, 1996) p.149

Chapter 18

Healing - Love

Love can be compared to warm melted chocolate cascading down like lava in a tiered fountain. Experiencing this slow moving, mouth watering display excites one's senses. It has a warmth you can feel as well as a delicious, tantalizing aroma. For chocolate lovers, this bubbling and roiling mass is both soothing and elating at the same time. The excitement of tasting, smelling, and touching the chocolate only adds to the pleasure. We know from previous experience that wonderful taste, and even though it may contain untold amounts of unhealthy ingredients we still find it irresistible.

Love also invokes pleasure to the senses and we experience an intimacy that both engulfs and edifies. Loving in the Spirit has a feeling and movement that reaches deep into the heart of both giver and recipient. The heart's desire is to embrace, acknowledge and release its flow. People receiving Holy Spirit's touch respond in a noticeable way as the power of love embraces and touches them. The outcome is sometimes very brief but can be profound. A kind word, smile or comment can deeply change the disposition of another.

"Too often we underestimate the power of a touch, a smile, a kind word, a listening ear, an honest compliment, or the smallest act of caring, all of which have the potential to turn a life around. It's overwhelming to consider the continuous opportunities there are to make our love felt."[72]

That level of sensory delight we can meet in chocolate in the natural world is something we also desire of the supernatural realm. We want to see, smell and taste the goodness of the Lord. Unfortunately, the ego too often will not allow love to have its way.

Love stands alone when initiated by the Holy Spirit. His work is the basis of our spiritual giftings. Love represents more than a word because it is the foundation of spiritual life in Jesus Christ.

© 2010 Doreen S. Barber

Love is an action word; it has its own passion and gives meaning to our existence.

Love has no hooks, demands, or expectations except for the highest good of the recipient.

Love is complete and inclusive.

Love from the heart is precious yet renewable. The more it has given away, the more it is replenished.

It breathes life with meaning in the heart and the spirit of those who receive it.

It is what we do for people that will be remembered; not what religion we preached.

---

[72] Leo Buscaglia, Born For Love (Ballantine Books, New York, 1992) p.232

Love, genuine, travels in many streams, resulting in emo-
    tional, physical, or spiritual wholeness.
Love is a gift we give to people.
Love doesn't ask for a fee nor seek a repayment.
Love is given without strings attached.
Love willingly wants to be obedient to the Master's call.
Love embraces all character flaws and attitudes.

Mother Teresa said, "Every time you smile at someone,
it is an action of love, a gift to that person, a beautiful
thing."

Whenever we feel His touch, the movement within is
permanent and evermore life changing. We begin to mature and grow more into His likeness by the power of love.
Having been nurtured in love by Holy Spirit to depths
unplumbed by our humanity, He initiates the process of
knowing Jesus, His unfailing love, and trusting Him to
bring about the completion He desires.

Jesus never countenanced evil, although he did stand
ready to forgive it. Somehow, he gained the reputation as
a lover of sinners.[73]

The Trinity operates in the realm of truth, light and
clarification. We are limited as finite beings and not able
to fully understand or realize the awesome spirituality of
God, though the expanse of creation gives us a glimpse
into the magnitude of the Creator.

"For us human beings love is a power which achieves
the incredible. Love is the greatest force on earth. But
with God love is more than something. With God love is
someone, a person. And that is the Third Person of the

---

[73] Philip Yancey, What's So Amazing About Grace?", (Zondervan
Publishing House, Grand Rapids, Michigan 49530, 1997)p. 144

Blessed Trinity. He is the miraculous love who unites the Father and the Son into a perfect unity."[74]

As we look at all created human beings we see each has a soul (mind, will and emotions) that governs and controls behaviors. We are created beings but with spirit choices. We often come to the conclusion there are no changes are needed in our relationship with the Lord only to realize He knows and examines our spirits with truth. In (Proverbs 16:2 ESV) "All the ways of a man are pure in his own eyes, but the Lord weighs the spirit."

Jesus declared after His resurrection that He is *life* by the following verse: And He said to them, "O foolish ones, and slow of heart to believe all that the prophets have spoken! Was it not necessary that the Christ should suffer these things and enter into his glory? And beginning with Moses and all the Prophets, he interpreted to them in all the Scriptures the things concerning himself." (Luke 24:25-27 ESV) The study of scripture is very important to develop our faith, nurture us in growth but it should never replace our personal connectedness with Him. God is offering us a relationship. Interacting perpetually, meditating on His word, praying and listening for His voice are integral parts of our daily walk. Having our life in Him combines intimacy with open communication, sharing all our feelings, griefs, upsets, questions and disappointments. This allows us to express ourselves freely without the threat of judgment. There is then a mutual respect and kindness expressed in this relationship with our Lord but also our friend. "No longer do I call you servants, for the servant does not know what his master is doing; but I have called you friends, for all that I have

---

[74] Peter G. van Breemen, S.J. As Bread That Is Broken (Dimension Books Inc., Denville, New Jersey, 1974) p.174

heard from my Father I have made known to you." (John 15:15 ESV)

Joy and laughter shared in a progressive growing union.

A team of professional people passed out this question to a group of 4 to 8 year-olds. "What does love mean?" Consider the wisdom of this child's reply.

"When my grandmother got arthritis, she couldn't bend over and paint her toenails anymore. So my grand-father does it for her all the time, even when his hands got arthritis too. That's love" Rebecca – age 8

Author and lecturer Leo Buscaglia once talked about a contest he was asked to judge. The purpose of the contest was to find the most caring child. The winner was a four-year-old child whose next-door neighbor was an elderly gentleman who had recently lost his wife.

Upon seeing the man cry, the little boy went into the old gentleman's yard, climbed onto his lap, and just sat there. When his Mother asked what he had said to the neighbor, the little boy said, "Nothing, I just helped him cry"

One of the greatest lessons learned is that love comes from the heart; it is spoken from the heart and is experienced in the heart.

Love is healing.
Love is special, Love is sweet,
Love is what makes life complete
Love is giving, love is kind,
Love is joy and peace of mind
Love is laughter, seldom tears,
Sharing, caring, through the years
Love is more than words to express,
But mostly, love is happiness.
Love, The Pantry Hospitality corp., 19

Chapter 19

The Demonic, Legalism, and Religiosity

Those who claim to know Jesus but do not have a personal relationship with Him often misrepresent the Lord. This misrepresentation becomes heartbreaking once we realize Him who we love has been given a bad rap. If we are not close enough to defend Him, then lifting these people up in prayer is the only available option, but also the most beneficial. To know of God is diametrically and profoundly opposite to knowing God, and there are countless numbers of people who fall in this category. In them, there is a seeking after spirituality, but never finding the author of Life. One involves the intellect, but the other involves the heart.

How can we demonstrate our personal intimate relationship with the Lord?

Many believers and unbelievers focus on material possessions in their existence. These are neither what He died for nor the objects of His pleasure. The items that give us comfort are certainly of value, but they can also become all- consuming and distracting to a fault. The amount of time spent in the pursuit of our pleasures are often disproportionate to the time we spend with the Lord. It would benefit us more to spend time examining our own hearts as we work out our salvation with fear and trembling, living sober lives and nurturing of our relationship with Jesus. (Philippians 2:12 ESV) Daily we need to foster our relationship with God, not being content with past resplendence. We are to be His light. This world is hungry to see tangible realities of love.

There is truth in the old saying, "actions speak louder than words." (Author Unknown) We know that ninety percent of communication is non-verbal. The 'spectators' or unbelievers are constantly watching our actions to find chinks in our armor, and this is important because statistics reveal that a high percentage of people come to the Lord through an acquaintance or a friend. Our thoughts and actions need constant supervision as we easily forget ourselves and slide into legalistic rules, rules that are often borrowed from religious organizations and are added to the ones we already erroneously believe.

"Leo Tolstoy, who battled legalism all his life, understood the weaknesses of a religion based on externals. The title of one of his books says it well: *The Kingdom of God is Within You.* According to Tolstoy, all religious systems tend to promote external rules, or moral-ism. In contrast, Jesus refused to define a set of rules that his followers could then fulfill with a sense of satisfaction. One can never arrive..."[75]

Jesus entered the synagogue on the Sabbath where he saw a man with a withered hand. He was being watched by the Pharisees to see if He would heal on the Sabbath so that they might accuse Him of wrongdoing. And He

[75] Philip Yancey, What's So Amazing About Grace? (Zondervan Publishing House, grand Rapids, Michigan 49530, 1997) p.180-181

said to them "is it lawful on the Sabbath to do good or to do harm, to save life or to kill?" But they were silent. And he looked around at them with anger, grieved at their hardness of heart..." (Mark 3:4-5 ESV) Legalism and religiosity destroys compassion, kindness, care and even the miraculous. The previous passage illustrates the legalism and hardness of heart that the religious leaders and Herodians held against Jesus, so that after this incident, they held counsel together on how to destroy him.

Believers live with a continuous dichotomy between freedom and conformity. The desire to be accepted by our peers is intense. We choose daily whether to follow a God-fearing devout pattern or legalistic humanist standards. (Matthew 22:36-40 ONM) "Teacher, which is the greatest commandment in the Torah (Teaching)? And He said to him, "You will love the Lord your God with your whole heart and with your whole being and with your whole mind: this is the greatest and first commandment," and the second is like it, "you will love your neighbor as yourself. The whole Torah (Teaching) and the Prophets are hanging on these two commandments." Freedom is desired but conformity is comfortable. We balance our choices and their consequences as we determine our daily walk with God.

Our hearts can be like the hub of a wheel that is bumping along the road until we realize we have a flat tire. There is a pressing need to stop the car and examine its wheels. For the sake of our purity, we would like our hearts to control all our actions, but sadly these actions mostly indicate the truthful reality of our depravity.

Self-examination in the light of Holy Spirit exposes true motives. Motives around self-interest and conditioned love can expose our core being and the ultimate source of what is in conflict with Holy Spirit.

The areas of hurt, disappointment, anger, resentment, abuse etc...give legal right to the enemy as he whispers, prods and pokes us to demonstrate unkind and inappropriate behaviors. This is an area of discussion that generates untold discourse as to whether a Christian can be demonized or not. It is disturbing to have worked with so many people who proclaim Jesus as Lord yet struggle with oppression by the demonic. Obstacles and hindrance in their daily lives keep them handcuffed from serving the Lord unreservedly. Not all personnel in ministry are willing to admit this demonic persecution exists and, therefore, take other approaches to healing. Just as Jesus healed and cast out demons in His ministry (Mark 1:34) the same power through Holy Spirit is available to all believers today.

It has been well said that "Legalism makes apostasy easy."[76]

Legalism is one area that is very active and alive in religious systems today. Sometimes, the most meaningless act can cause an uproar. Simply clapping in church, the raising of hands, wearing what is deemed incorrect apparel, the use of makeup or men sporting shoulder length hair can be censored. The legalistic or religious react to what they think is nonspiritual. The impiety of such actions then causes a tumult of negative behaviors in some parishioners. Divisions among believing brothers and sisters have occurred over issues as trivial as the color of a new carpet. Such acts parallel those of the Pharisees protesting the healing Jesus did on the Sabbath. Such

---

[76] Philip Yancey, What's So Amazing About Grace? (Zondervan Publishing House, grand Rapids, Michigan 49530, 1997) p.189

conflict can become even more severe over doctrinal issues with sides forming and becoming entrenched.

People with a sense of righteousness or worthiness in the sight of God that comes from keeping the law as they understand it are easily provoked. Their legalistic attained position gives them a false sense of authority and dominance. Piousness frequently inflicts offenses causing injury resulting in severed relationships.

Unbelievers recognize the hypocrisy as they observe these shortcomings. Identification is immediate to their own lives and judgment is quickly leveled.

Below the cross of Jesus we all stand, hands empty and hearts willing. The music is playing and we want to hear every note and then dance to its rhythm. David, filled with joy, heard the music and danced before the Lord. (2 Samuel 6:14 ESV)

The challenge is to become free of all encumbrances or worthlessness that try to hinder us from dancing before the King with joy at our great salvation.

(Psalm 51:10 NIV) "Create in me a clean heart, oh God, and renew a right (steadfast) spirit within me." His desire is to make us whole with complete freedom to serve Him. Calling on Him to create in us a clean heart is asking Him to do in us the work of renewal and restoration. In (Psalm 51:6 ESV) "...truth in the inward being....wisdom in the secret heart."

The forces in this world pale in comparison to the mighty and supreme power of Jesus. Recognizing areas of demonic activity can heighten our due diligence, causing us to seek the Lord, obtaining hope and strength from Him. The right to claim the freedom given to us after Christ's resurrection is there for the asking. "Rejoice always I say rejoice." (Philippians 4:4 ESV) As His children, we claim triumphantly the delight and exuberant happiness that belongs to us.

The Lord is preparing to return for a bride who is ready—fine linen, clean and white, this the righteousness of saints. (Revelation. 19:8 KJV) Through His glorious love He is cleansing, restoring and fashioning our hearts with extraordinary compassion and grace.

One of our frequent prayers needs to be: Jesus I am unable to do this on my own. Lord send me your light and faithful care. (Psalm 43:3) I need your guidance, please teach me your way.

"So we do not lose heart. Though our outer self is wasting away, our inner self is being renewed day by day." (2 Corinthians 4:15 ESV)

Obstacles set before us, either in the demonic, in legalism or in religiosity are but mere hiccups along life's path with the Lord. Under His grace and guiding eye, a relief from the impediments of entrapment or interference is only a breath away. The enemy would like us to believe He can entrap us, but under the Lord's power, he is thwarted.

Einstein said, "The significant problems we face cannot be solved at the same level of thinking which created them."[77]

The renewing of our heart daily changes our perspective, motivating us to attain and grasp all that He has planned and purposed. An old saying is, 'hope springs eternal.' The eternal is in Jesus!

---

[77] Wayne W. Dyer, There's a Spiritual Solution To Every Problem (Harper Collins,, 10 East 53rd Street, New York, N.Y. 10022, 2001) p.40

Chapter 20

The Law of Love

The word law conjures up many images from the legal systems of the world. Bonding to the rituals of legalism in the spiritual realm hampers freedom. In most countries, the legal system offers protection from the wrong doing of criminals against its law-abiding people. On the other hand, legalism in a religious or spiritual system, through traditions or rules, attempts to restrict our gained freedoms, which negatively affect our beliefs and faith.

Here a response is needed, as the forces that try to break down our gained freedoms have to be challenged. For example, some churches require ladies to wear hats or head apparel when entering a church or cathedral. Does this action warrant discipline by leadership?

This kind of legalism is an example of a man made rule that only serves to hinder the gospel message. Issues such as these are continually before Christians who wish to follow obedient, also many sincere parishioners fall victim to legalism. They may feel their only option is to withdraw altogether. Fear, then, becomes a major factor in the life of the believer. As in this case, fear of confrontation with its unknown consequences subsumes what ought to be their reason to be in fellowship with the body of believers.

Responding to emotional or contemptuous behavior only escalates the powers of negativity. The person being confronted by opposition may internalize the offenses causing hurt, rejection and injury. Likely this injury will bring no immediate response that brings reconciliation or harmony. Forgiveness is the first step to take. Then, remaining in prayer, resting along with waiting on the Lord for direction will allow us to remain in peace.

We recognize that law in any culture is a commandment, decree, or edict formulated to govern citizens for the good of that society. For the majority of people it is understood as necessary to help rule including manage a population that needs guidelines with boundaries. Often the benefits of any law will diminish as it outgrows the purpose of why it was first initiated. A legal instrument may start with one aim and continue on for another. For example, trying to live up to or under the letter of the law in the rabbinic tradition of the Old Testament commandments meant following six hundred and thirteen rules.

The daily choice of doing the greater good in and for love is also a choice against legalism. Such choices can be confusing when expecting to attain fulfillment through the Mosaic commandments or laws, but the grace of sacrifice and forgiveness is for the highest good of love. An example would be in the O.T. There, God orders Abraham to kill his son Isaac. (Genesis 22- ESV Study Bible) This was his only son whom he loved. At the last moment, the Lord provided a ram as sacrifice and Isaac is spared. Abraham was stopped from murdering his son but the intent of his heart was to kill him as directed by God. Following this act of obedience God said "I will surely bless you, and I will surely multiply your offspring as the stars of heaven and as the sand that is on the seashore. And your off spring shall possess the gate of his enemies, and in your offspring shall all the nations of the earth be blessed, because you have obeyed my voice." (v.17-18) His lineage is followed through the Bible to King Jesus who will rule over Gentiles and all nations.

Fortunately most of us will not have to make such a difficult choice in this life, although obedience to His voice is always an absolute. Obedience to the measure of faith we have been given requires an action. (Romans 1:5-6 ESV) "Through whom we have received grace and apostleship to bring about the obedience of faith for the sake of His name among all the nations, including you who are called to belong to Jesus Christ." (Romans 12:3-4 ONM) further states: "For I say, through the grace that has been given to me, to everyone who is among you, not to think too highly of yourselves beyond which it is necessary to think, but to think to put a moderate estimate of yourself, in the same manner as God divided to each a measure of faith." This not only applies to saving faith received but the continuation of faith that brings about obedience. This action brings about transformed lives consistently obedient to God for the sake of His name.

There are other ethical love choices that we face almost daily. The hard choices, unless backed up by the Lord's Commandments, will leave us asking including speculating. How do we determine the best choice between an absolute command and an exemption to view the higher priorities love? Our day to day lives include decisions that can lead us to question the law of love.

How does the law of love operate and are we then held accountable for ill choices?

"If I (God) take away the consequences of people's choices I destroy the possibility of love. Love that is forced is no love at all."[78] The 'I' in this quote refer to God, although a fictional story, The Shack, it has great depth in representing the heart of God.

Making difficult choices leads us back to the Jesus who is always waiting to give His guidance. "Do not be anxious about anything, but in everything, by prayer and petition, with thanksgiving, present your request to God." (Philippians 3:6 NIV) The cross is a marker signifying the back of sin has been broken. Choices now determine where love will take us. Love is expressed in the free exercise of choice.

At times we will be walking a fine line in determining the most loving action to take between choices given; therefore choose what is the most loving.

"...I was told to read "The Rime of the Ancient Mariner."...I opened the book directly to the words "He prayeth best, who loveth best/All things both great and small;/For the dear God who loveth us,/He made and loveth all." I realized I was being told that there are no exceptions - if you're going to love, you have to love everyone."[79]

The law of love required is this: (Matthew 22:37-40 ESV) And he said to him, "You shall love the Lord your God with all your heart and with all your soul and with all your mind. This is the great and first commandment.

[78] William P. Young, The Shack (Windblown Media, 4680 Calle Norte, Newbury Park,CA, 2007) p.190

[79] Bernie S. Siegel, M.D. Peace, Love & Healing (HarperCollins Publishers Inc., 10 East 53rd. Street, New York, NY 10022) p.69

And the second is like it: You shall love your neighbor as yourself. On these two commandments depend all the Law and the Prophets." The law of love declares total devotion of the whole person, not compartments of the individual.

Is there any possible command more important than this one?

No man-made law can ever be as essential as this one. Perhaps this is where we are led astray. When the law of love is not the principal priority in our hearts and minds, other laws in earthly life accept or supersede it, as a consequence, dictate our behavior consequences. Because their influence is so powerful, if we fail to examine the religious systems of our lives they will undoubtedly lead us astray into legalistic behaviors. The religiosity exhibited even in well-intentioned people can sidetrack our relationship with the Lord, a relationship of great honor that requires our rigorous protection.

"Salvation in Christ with the presence of Holy Spirit brought us freedom from condemnation, guilt, sin, death, the old covenant, and blindness, and to the gospel. We have access to the loving presence of God." (2 Corinthians 3:17 ESV)

"I learned grace by being graced."[80]

Many of us take a wrong turn for a time before we stumble, fall as well as get bruised. When we get up and dust ourselves off, we ask for His mercy and grace. It is in those times His love fills our hearts and we are able to gain insight into our errors. Once having learned to always be before Him, we are less likely to find ourselves face down in the dirt each time before we call for help.

---

[80] Philip Yancey, What's So Amazing About Grace? (Zondervan Publishing House, grand Rapids, Michigan 49530, 1997) p. 37

The core of our hearts and how we choose to live indicates our personal truth. Spiritually, we must walk this road by ourselves, being accountable to one and only one person, Jesus. Our accountability and interaction with humanity is directly reflected back to Jesus, who relied solely on His Father for direction, always doing His will. Likewise, this is the same for us, to be totally dependent on Jesus.

"You were intended out of love, you must be love in order to intend."[81]

The law of love is stated in (Galatians 5:13-15 ESV) "For you were called to freedom, brothers. Only do not use your freedom as an opportunity for the flesh, but through love serve one another. For the whole law is fulfilled in one word: you shall love your neighbor as yourself. But if you bite and devour one another, watch out that you are not consumed by one another."

Our calling is distinct - avoid falling into external (fleshly) or worldly activities when serving. Acting in love, however, dissipates disagreements as a result dissensions that may grow into destructive actions or behaviors.

---

[81] Dr. Wayne W. Dyer, The Power of Intention (Hay House Inc., P.O. Box 5100, Carlsbad, CA 92018-5100, 2004) p.50

Chapter 21

Love: The Final Word

J ust as the final chapter is written on love—so how we
loved in His name will be the concluding words written as the accounting of our earthly life ends. This
accounting is taking place now and will be presented
to us at the last reading.

There is no other greater and more meaningful purpose on earth than to be ushered into the Kingdom, to
love the Lord, and demonstrate His love to others. We are
told to go and make disciples of all nations. (Matthew.
28:19 ESV) This fulfills His plan, purpose and calling for
our lives. His love was freely given for our redemption.
His blood being spilled on the ground along with His
body bruised for our transgressions. The resurrection declared to the world that death had no hold on him. Jesus
declared "all authority in heaven and earth has been
given to me." (Matthew 28: 18 ESV)

A sempiternal (endless and infinite) number of
books have been written on the subject of what Jesus did
demonstrating love. (John 21:25 ESV) "Jesus did many
other things as well. If every one of them were written
down, I suppose that even the whole world would not

have room for the books that would be written." Many are the libraries in the world that could not hold the numerous miracles and teachings of Jesus. We are only, by inspiration, given a synopsis of His life events.

The greatest gift we have been given is to experience the Divine Love that had come at the supreme price-His own death. To partake in this supernatural, spiritual kingdom requires but a simple step forward. Believing and accepting Him as Savior who is the Resurrection and the Life. We then become the King's most precious child, moreover the spirit transition and transformation begins. The exchange for His Spirit transcends all our known senses into the light of His crowning glory. As one of His children we have been given the privilege of entering into His Kingdom and all the riches it offers. (John 3: 13-15 ONM) "And no one has ascended to heaven except the One Who has descended from heaven, the Son of Man. And just as Moses lifted up the serpent in the wilderness, so also it is necessary for the Son of Man to be lifted up, so that everyone who believes in Him would have eternal life." There is no other religion that offers such an inexplicable divine earthly life or eternal resting place.

Love is at the very core of this marvelous opportunity where the invitation is open to all along with a few simple words spoken from the heart. "Lord, I accept you as my Savior, come and live in my heart. Forgive me for my sins that I have committed against you. Thank-you." The majestic life-giving exchange has now taken place. We enter into the beginnings of the most infinite and magnificent love relationship we will ever know. It is a love relationship too marvelous for words. The Holy Spirit placed within our hearts furthermore sealed with the Creator's signet of love. His love captures our heart.

Receiving our pardon is the greatest and most awe-inspiring gift ever given. The exchange is not complicated if we continue to open our hearts broader and deeper to Jesus because, the Holy Spirit will expand our love for Him. Kingdom works, signs and wonders will follow. There are not many ways, as some other religions or cults purport, to find God; there is one and only one way through Jesus Christ, the name given above all names! (John 14: 6 ESV)

As children and friends of Christ, trying to describe Him leaves us speechless in amazement and awe of His divinity. Human language is inadequate in describing His glory and majesty. Love, birthed in the truth of His existence, grows and matures under His watchful eye.

Unconditional or absolute divine love transcends our human awareness or natural comprehension. How can we possibly describe such a glorious, miraculous and divine gift deep within the heart?

© 2010 Doreen S. Barber
Love is a mystery, that will never, this side of heaven, be
     plumbed to its depth.
Love can move the largest obstacles, knows no limita-
     tions or handicaps.
Love always responds to the need of others.
Love does not dictate its own way.
Love is not led blindly along, but has the ingredients of
     care, insight, consideration and wisdom. Love consid-
     ers all requests and wisely responds.

Making choices based on love demands attention to His Spirit. Our only responsibility is to kindle passion for Him into a flame. "For this reason I remind you to fan into flame the gift of God, which is in you through the laying on of my hands, for God gave us a spirit not of fear but of power and love and self-control." (2 Timothy 1:6-7 ESV) The gift of His love and grace requests our attention to obedience, seeking, searching, worship and praise. Our duty is to chose daily where we place our thoughts and actions.

The Lord's heart is full of passion for his bride and he desires the most extravagant love affair with her. (Jude v. 20-21 ONM) "But you, beloved, as you build yourselves up in your most holy faith, praying in the Holy Spirit, you must continually keep yourselves in the love of God, anticipating the mercy of our Lord Y'shua Messiah for eternal life."

This writer states "As an inheritance, God the Father has promised the Son a church filled with believers whose spirits are ablaze with affections and adoration for Jesus."[82]

Those born of the Spirit of God are now given the opportunity to explore love to depths beyond what their imaginations can envision.

He will prompt the action and movement He wishes us to follow. Our choices are very critical, we must choose to be obedient or refuse His direction. Our hearts joined with Holy Spirit will do great works in His name, His love and power will be demonstrated in our lives.

"Any action that inhibits is not love. Love is only love when it liberates."[83]

As we are walking in His power and love to the degree that it captivates us will be the degree that will be

---

[82] Mike Bickle, Passion For Jesus (Creation House, 600 Rineharet Road, Lake Mary, FL 32746, 1993) p.72
[83] Leo Buscaglia, Born For Love, (Ballantine Books, New York, 1992) p.293

expressed to reach those around us. His Spirit will speak powerfully and undeniably into as well as from our hearts. Loving people with the prompting and heart transition of His Spirit will become effortless the more in love we are with Him.

"I am the Alpha and the Omega," says the Lord God, "who is and who was and who is to come, the Almighty." (Revelation 1:8 ESV) Alpha and omega (the first and last letters of the (Gk. Alphabet ESV Study Bible)

God initiated love to His creation through Jesus. All people will bow before the glorified Lord. Free will given to man through accepting choice allows us access into the Holy of Holies.

"Lord, make me an instrument of thy peace.
Where there is hatred, let me sow love.
Where there is injury, pardon.
Where there is doubt, faith.
Where there is despair, hope.
Where there is darkness, light.
Where there is sadness, joy.
O Divine Master,
Grant that I may not so much seek to be consoled as to
    console,
to be understood as to understand;
to be loved as to love.
For it is in giving that we receive.
It is in pardoning that we are pardoned.
It is in dying that we are born to eternal life.
Amen."
--Saint Francis of Assisi

Those who believe on the name of Jesus, who are brought into His kingdom of love, with grace that abounds, are the most fortunate blessed people in the world. They will know a life lived abundantly on earth and the guarantee of eternal love and living in His presence, walking in the light, truth and glory, face to face with the Lord forever.

(1 Peter 1:4 ESV) states: "to an inheritance that is imperishable, undefiled, and unfading, kept in heaven for you."

To exalt His name let our prayer be *"Father, where you have implanted us in this world and for the purposes of your choosing may you receive the honor and glory."* Amen.

Printed in the United States
By Bookmasters